For Team Members Only

For Team Members Only

Making Your Workplace Team Productive and Hassle-Free

Charles C. Manz
Christopher P. Neck
James Mancuso
Karen P. Manz

AMACOM
American Management Association
New York • Atlanta • Boston • Chicago • Kansas City • San Francisco • Washington, D.C.
Brussels • Mexico City • Tokyo • Toronto

Library of Congress Cataloging-in-Publication Data

For team members only : making your workplace team productive and
    hassle-free / Charles C. Manz . . . [et al.].
        p.   cm.
    Includes bibliographical references and index.
    ISBN 0-8144-7946-4 (pbk.)
    1. Teams in the workplace.   2. Self-directed work teams.
I. Manz, Charles C.
HD66.F65   1997
658.4'036—dc21   97-7127
                                                                  CIP

Printing number

10 9 8 7 6 5 4 3 2 1

To our primary team members in life:
Sandy, Lisa, Jim, *and* **Steve**
Jennifer
Christopher *and* **Katy**

TABLE OF CONTENTS

PREFACE

This book is for team members only. It is meant to be something you hold, read and re-read, and even take to your team for sharing. But mostly it is to be used by you alone, in quiet times. It is then that you can reflect upon your team and how well you and your team members contribute to it.

For Team Members Only directly focuses on team members and the challenges, issues, and concerns they tend to face. We have developed this book around the real-life experiences of team members, the wealth of literature on teams, and our own experience and expertise. We consolidated and analyzed multiple sources of data we had all collected in our field visits and consulting with numerous organizations that were struggling with team implementation and development. We looked for commonalities of concern as expressed in the comments made by team members in focus-group–type meetings or other small-group sessions. Team member experiences were our starting point.

Books on teams have flooded the market. Some of them discuss the needs of team members, but most focus on issues relevant to managers and human resources specialists. These books tend to be rather technical in style and fall outside the daily concerns of the typical team member. Our aim was to provide accessible information and tools to assist team members with their specific questions. We wanted to make this book a comfortable and useful learning tool. We wanted it to be provocative and enjoyable, and we also wanted to be creative with it. That's why you will find a mix of stories, cases, exercises, questions—and even poetry!

You have taken a critical step in picking up this book. You recognize that learning is crucial to being an effective team member. Ongoing learning is a daily task. There is so much to learn about how teams work, how to get along with team members, how to get work done, and how to keep up with the knowledge demanded by your work tasks.

Being an active learner is a healthy attribute of a team member. The learning can't be done all at once; rather, take small steps day by day. Relax, learn, and enjoy your team!

ACKNOWLEDGMENTS

We are grateful to many people who have been instrumental in enabling us to write this book. First, we appreciate the support of our publisher, AMACOM, and especially our editor, Mary Glenn. Chuck Manz and Chris Neck thank all the members of their universities, Arizona State University and Virginia Tech, respectively, who have supported their research and writing over the years, especially Larry Penley, Bill Glick, Richard Sorensen, and Jon Shepard. Chuck Manz also expresses his appreciation for the support of his new colleagues at the University of Massachusetts, where he will be the Charles and Janet Nirenberg Professor of Business Leadership beginning in the fall of 1997, especially Tom O'Brien, Tony Butterfield, Bob Marx, and Marc Weinberger.

There are many other colleagues we need to recognize. Hank Sims, Jr., who has collaborated with Chuck Manz for years, has had a major impact on many of the ideas presented in this book. Other important and influential colleagues include Greg Stewart, Vikas Anand, Richard Hackman, Ed Lawler, Mike Byerlein, Chris Argyris, Barry Macy, Richard Cherry, Janice Klein, Frank Shipper, Alan Cheney, Barry Bateman, Joe Hollis, Mary Connerley, Heidi Ream, and Ramesh Gulati. All of these people have significantly affected our thinking about teams.

We are grateful to many companies and their employees that have shared informal insights that helped guide our selection of topics and practical solutions to team member challenges in this book: Motorola, GM, Ford, Allied Signal, Sverdrup Technologies, Procter & Gamble, AES, Texas Instruments, IDS Financial Services, Charrette, W. L. Gore Associates, Lake Superior Paper, Digital Equipment Corporation, Honeywell, Paramax, Prudential, Mayo Clinic, MD Anderson Cancer Center, Josten's Learning, and the Center for the Study of Work Teams at the University of North Texas, among others.

Chris thanks his brother and sister, Brent and Heidi Neck, for their encouragement and support.

Finally, we thank one another. It has been a rewarding experience for each of us to be part of the author team, and we hope you will find the results of our efforts—this book—to be helpful and rewarding to you as well.

INTRODUCTION

Being a team member is hard work. It can be threatening, uncomfortable, and overwhelming at times—but it can also be a source of support, high rewards, and a vast learning experience about yourself and others.

How do you feel about being on a team? What do you like about it? What do you find most difficult about being a team member? Are there some things about teams that drive you crazy? Would you like to learn more about how to survive and thrive on a team? It is our hope that this book will be a practical guide for team members like you to help you cope and succeed in the world of teams.

Teamwork: Overview of the Book

Our primary work tasks as a team of authors were to figure out what information to include in this book and how to present it. We went through many of the same steps and processes you will read about. For the most part, we worked many miles apart from each other, except for two of the authors who are married to each other. Our communication, self-leadership, and problem solving were especially important. We hope our teamwork will help build your teamwork.

This book contains short, skill-based units targeted at the kinds of basic knowledge and concerns confronting team members. For example, we talk about how you can communicate with both assertiveness and cooperation on

your team, how you can help build trust, and how to motivate and lead yourself on an empowered team.

Every team member struggles with the tension between the needs and desires of herself and those of the
other team members. You have an impact on your team,
and your team has an impact on you. An important philo-
sophical stance of this book is that each team member
works to strengthen the quality and balance of the "me"
and "we" in the team experience, so we address issues that
team members can work on individually, such as dealing
effectively with personal stress on the job, but that have an
impact on the team as a whole.

We think it is important for team members to work
together and support each other, especially when one
member is struggling or is frustrated. What we call "take
it to the team" is our way of encouraging a team member
to approach the others for clarification, problem solving,
or other support. Many units in this book suggest some
level of team involvement, and we give guidance in many
cases to "take it to the team" for discussion and action.

The main issues we talk about—Teamthink, Team
Leadership, Team Self-Leadership, Team Talk, and Team
Problem Solving—are presented so that you have the opportunity to think about their effect on you and the life of
your team. We include lots of opportunities for focusing
on your own experiences and thinking through situations
common to teams. There is ample space to jot down your
reactions and responses if you choose. Questions for reflection, personal assessment, and suggested steps for taking action, if desired, are offered continually.

Teamthink is a process of team decision making that
enables members to combine their individual experiences
and ideas into a synergistic, integrated whole. Several of
these units deal with the problems of *groupthink*, the tendency for groups to become overly conforming and ineffective in their decision making. Our emphasis is on how
to balance individual skills and abilities with cooperation
in the team. We use the term *teamthink* to identify the positive situation where unique individual experiences and

strengths are preserved and developed and then combined for the good of the whole group.

Team Leadership and *Team Self-Leadership* refer to the team member's capacity to influence others effectively, as well as his own self-leadership. These complementary leadership skills enable the team to enjoy the benefits of both competent individual members and effective teamwork. Several units address these processes of self-leadership (leading oneself) and SuperLeadership (leading others to lead themselves); others address the formal role of the team leader.

Team Talk involves a variety of effective communication techniques that allow for an open, productive, and conflict-managed arena for the exchange of ideas within the team. A variety of units spell out specific skills you can use to improve your personal communication. Other units focus on how you can help build the communication skills of your team members. Special attention is given to trust building, a critical ingredient for healthy communication.

Several units address *Team Problem Solving:* the important team decision-making and problem-solving process. Some specific application areas include dealing with problem team members, learning how to disagree in constructive ways, clarifying what the team wants to accomplish in the problem-solving process, and working toward compromise. Ethics and time management are also discussed.

Team Play, the last stop in this book, is a team-building exercise for you to have fun with as you get to know your team members better. The life on your team needs a mix of teamwork and team play.

What Are Teams?

Teams—self-directed teams, self-managing teams, and high-performance teams—are a new work design innovation that has swept across the country, and the rest of the world. Estimates are that 40 to 50 percent of the workforce could be in some kind of empowered work team environment by the turn of the century.

The introduction of empowered work teams into the workplace represents perhaps the most important new organization development since the Industrial Revolution. Teams have already demonstrated their ability to make major contributions to organizations in a variety of industries. Increased productivity, higher product and service quality, a better quality of work life for employees, and reduced costs, turnover, and absenteeism are among the more salient payoffs.

Usually team members have an increased amount of responsibility and control. Teams perform many of the tasks that used to be the responsibility of management, such as conducting meetings, solving technical and personal problems, and making a wide range of decisions on many issues, including performance methods and deciding who will complete which task. Teams that are successful are those that possess the skills, equipment, and supplies they need to perform their work well.

The best teams tend to have capable and committed members who successfully combine their skills and knowledge for the good of the team. The challenge for teams is to accept and appreciate the unique contributions that each member can make while effectively combining individual member contributions for the good of the team. The key to team success is the creation of synergy—the condition whereby team members together accomplish significantly more than they could if they acted on their own. (A mathematical example of synergy is $1 + 1 + 1 = 5$.) This definition fits quite well with the widely used acronym TEAM—Together Everyone Achieves More. Teams are best when their members have strong individual skills and strong team skills.

Team Types and Stages

Teams tend to develop their own personality depending on the people on the team and the kind of work they perform.

Moreover, each team is unique, and the way it appears on the surface may not be the best way to assess its effectiveness. There is no ideal type of team. Some teams are easygoing, and everyone seems to get along well; over time, though, the members may find that they fall into a rut and don't challenge the way they work in order to improve. Other teams experience a lot of conflict between members, yet this conflict can stimulate creative problem solving.

Teams form for different purposes and varying amounts of time, and they can have a changing membership. You may be on one team or several teams simultaneously. You may be on a temporary task force type of team or permanently assigned to one. You may be on a team of three or four who work together everyday, or you may be on what your organization calls a team—with 1,000 members you see once a year at a company picnic. Some teams meet only weekly or monthly. You may be on a team where members depend on each other for life-or-death decision making and efficient teamwork, as in a hospital emergency room, or you may be on a team of independent sales representatives where you rarely meet with team members and you are mostly faceless and voiceless to the others.

Part of what makes teams so different is their stage of development. The best-known breakdown of team development identifies four stages:

1. **Forming,** when the team first comes together and tries to begin working as a team
2. **Storming,** when the team experiences early difficulty in the transition to teamwork and a great deal of conflict and struggle surfaces
3. **Norming,** when the team begins to work out internal shared understandings (norms) of how best to work together and members begin to follow these guidelines
4. **Performing,** when the members learn how to combine their efforts effectively and begin to function as a well-coordinated team[1]

The introduction of teams is not a painless process. In fact, typically work operations get worse before improvements are enjoyed as the bugs are worked out of the new system. For team members, the move to teams can be difficult and frightening. Teams require learning a whole new set of skills and being responsible to everyone on the team, not just a boss, as in traditional organizations.

Maintaining a strong team is hard work. There are always new challenges, new team members to assimilate, new work tasks to learn, or perhaps new products or new customers to deal with. Building trust, managing stress, striving for efficiency and quality, and balancing team members' individual needs with the needs of the team are ongoing. Communication is a full-time job in itself.

It's easy to see why teams differ so much. Among the many variables are the team members themselves, who help shape the life of a team.

Understanding Your Team

Understanding what teams are about and how they work is important for team members. Teams have been around long enough for us to learn how they typically develop and succeed. It is always helpful to talk with other teams within your organization to learn from their experiences, and plenty of good books tell the stories of various companies, associations, and other organizations, such as schools and hospitals, that have moved to teams. We encourage you to continue watching and learning from other teams.

Nevertheless, we believe the best starting point for learning more about teams is your own team. Your best learning comes from your own experiences. Let's take a moment to focus on your team. Think about the following questions and how they help shape the story of your team.

◇ My Team Story ◇

Answer these questions about your team. If you are a member of multiple teams, focus on the team that demands your greatest time or energy.

1. When was your team organized? _____

2. How many members are on the team? _____

3. If your team has a name, what is it? _____

4. What is the purpose of your team? _____

_____

5. On the average, how much face-to-face interaction do you have with team members?

_____ Minute by minute   _____ Hourly
_____ Daily   _____ Weekly/biweekly
_____ Monthly   _____ Very infrequently

6. How many of your current team members were on this team a year ago?

_____ None   _____ Between a quarter
_____ Less than a quarter   and a half
                            _____ Over half

7. What tasks do *you* do?
_____ The same as everyone else
_____ Team leader or facilitator
_____ Specialized work that no one else does
_____ Other (explain or give details)_____

_____

_____

8. Check the response that you think best characterizes your team members.

All	Some	A Few	None	My team members
⎯⎯	⎯⎯	⎯⎯	⎯⎯	Trust each other.
⎯⎯	⎯⎯	⎯⎯	⎯⎯	Pitch in whatever way to get the job done.
⎯⎯	⎯⎯	⎯⎯	⎯⎯	Share work-related information.
⎯⎯	⎯⎯	⎯⎯	⎯⎯	Address a problem when it arises.
⎯⎯	⎯⎯	⎯⎯	⎯⎯	Are concerned about the quality of their work.
⎯⎯	⎯⎯	⎯⎯	⎯⎯	Really listen to each other.
⎯⎯	⎯⎯	⎯⎯	⎯⎯	Feel comfortable voicing an opinion.
⎯⎯	⎯⎯	⎯⎯	⎯⎯	Give compliments and encouragement to each other.
⎯⎯	⎯⎯	⎯⎯	⎯⎯	Are committed to the team.
⎯⎯	⎯⎯	⎯⎯	⎯⎯	Are competent to do the required tasks.
⎯⎯	⎯⎯	⎯⎯	⎯⎯	Value other team members' contributions.
⎯⎯	⎯⎯	⎯⎯	⎯⎯	Understand our team's priorities and objectives.

9. What do you like best about your team? _____

_____

10. What do you like least about your team? _____

_____

Think about your answers. Did you come to any new insights or understandings? How did this exercise make you feel? Now take about five or ten minutes to share your team story with a trusted friend or relative but without using individual team member names. If you do not want to discuss this, try writing down your own team story.

The ABC's of Team Membership

In the "My Team Story" exercise you were asked to develop *your* team story, not your *team's* story. What is the difference? If your team members had completed the same exercise, do you think they would have the same story as yours? Probably not. In fact, we bet that you would have as many different team stories as the number of team members.

If you were asked to write your *team's* story, how would that be different? What information would you need for completing it? If only two of your team members contributed to the writing, would you feel confident that they could tell the whole team story? If all team members contributed to the writing, would you have greater confidence that a more realistic and accurate story would be told? Your *team's* story would need a description reflecting the variety of views of all your team members.

The issue we are dealing with here is the "me" "we" perspectives necessary for effective team membership. This means you need to focus on your own needs as well as those of your team members, and it is important to be aware of the uniqueness and strength of both perspectives. Every team member struggles with the tension between his needs and desires and those of the other team members. And there are multiple perspectives on a team at any given time, reflecting its varied members. You have an impact on your team, and your team has an impact on you.

Some of the most important ingredients necessary for a healthy team atmosphere go beyond the knowledge and skills we have only touched on in this Introduction. For example, you will be more helpful to your team if you look for the commonalities you have with others instead of the differences. Be patient with yourself and your team members. Take risks, try to be comfortable with the unknown, and have faith and confidence in the others.

◇ The Empowered Team Member Alphabet Game ◇

You may have played a version of this game as a child or recently if you have children or grandchildren. Think of values or characteristics suggested by a letter of the alphabet that identifies the ideal empowered team member. Using single words or phrases, write as many down as you can think of that begin with each letter. We have made some suggestions to help you start. You may want to work on this by yourself or with a team member. Have fun with this game!

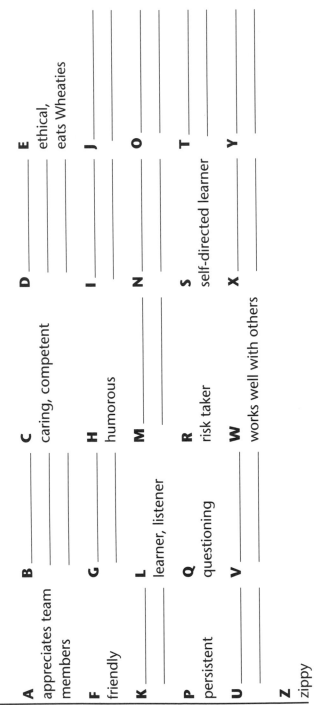

A
appreciates team members

B
_____

C
caring, competent

D
_____
_____
_____

E
ethical,
eats Wheaties

F
friendly

G
_____
_____

H
humorous

I
_____

J
_____

K
_____

L
learner, listener

M
_____

N
_____

O
_____

P
persistent

Q
questioning

R
risk taker

S
self-directed learner

T
_____

U
_____

V
_____

W
works well with others

X
_____

Y
_____

Z
zippy

To help you clarify how team members can be most helpful to their teams and to themselves in the process, try the "The Empowered Team Member Alphabet Game" on the facing page. Above all, develop a positive attitude about working on a team.

If you are looking for a challenge and adventure, you don't have to go on safari in Africa. Just go to work on a team!

After you have completed this game, reflect on the words listed. Are there areas where you can work to become a more empowered team member? Keep reading; this book will give you support and guidance in that direction.

A Team

There is a simple word
That can help you achieve your dream.
It's a secret to your success.
The word is simply "team."

"What is the meaning of this word?"
Is a question you might ask.
It involves an extensive effort
Towards accomplishing a task.

Not from a single person
Rather, by a coordinated group;
A process of working with others
That can bear lots of fruit.

To clarify the essence
Of what this noun relays,
Please listen to this story;
See what it has to say.

There was an aspiring woman
Given a sailboat for a gift.
So she headed out to the beach
With enthusiasm and her skiff.

After hours and hours of working alone
And struggling with all her might,
The boat never really moved;
She just couldn't get it right.

So she decided to invite some others
To help her complete this mission.
People who would navigate a yacht
With much skill and precision.

They quickly became a cohesive unit,
Communicating and giving their best,
With complete trust in each other,
The group focused on its quest.

Then an amazing thing occurred;
You could tell by the members' grin.
The vessel glided across the ocean;
They had finally "caught the wind."

The message in this nautical ode
Is that in order to prevail
When you don't succeed the first time,
You should never "take down the sail."

Rather, a change in your approach may be required
To make your vision a reality.
Working alone may not be the answer,
A team effort—could be the key.

So as you strive for excellence at home and work,
Remember again and again,
A team can conquer what an individual can't;
A team can "catch the wind." [2]

— Christopher P. Neck

1

TEAMTHINK

A process of team decision making and problem solving that enables members to combine their individual experiences and ideas into a synergistic whole

Breaking the Mold
Teamthink or Groupthink?
Balancing "Me" With "We"
A Win-Win Team Attitude

◪ BREAKING THE MOLD ◪

We have found that many of the people with whom we work, whether in a university, industrial, or business setting, have an initial resistance to working in teams. When faced with a difficult problem to solve many argue that they would rather do it alone. Their reasons for wanting to work alone include:

"I can get the job done more quickly by myself."

"I trust myself more than I trust others."

"Other people may be satisfied with less than I am."

"I don't want to run every decision by everyone else before I act on it."

"I don't want to adjust my schedule to fit other people."

"I think I know more than they do, so why should I compromise. Everybody knows that a camel is a horse put together by a committee."

"Why should I take the trouble to learn other people's jobs and not get paid more for it?"

Granted, these reasons all have some merit, and perhaps you have made a comment similar to one of them. (We would not be surprised to learn that.) Working alone is based on a strong tradition. It stems from early childhood when we were resistant to sharing and had to be encouraged to do so. Individualism was further reinforced throughout our schooling when we were repeatedly admonished to do our own work. Is it any wonder that you or I or some of our team members may resist self-managed work teams as the way to function in the workplace? Individualism is the mold in which most of us were patterned.

The individualistic tendency to trust self more than the team is a challenge we must address and a mold that must be broken if we are to reap the benefits of teaming. Going it alone may have been the rugged approach of the autocratic leaders of the past, but collaboration and team-work is the progressive direction for the future.

In matters involving judgment, the product of informed group thinking is typically superior to an informed individual thinking by herself. Let's examine some of the reasons through statements by many people who have participated in our seminars:

"Team members represent five to ten times more life experience that any one individual has."

"Two heads are better than one."

"The whole is often greater than the sum of the parts. Teams often come up with better ideas than one person would have dreamed of alone."

"Team members can often challenge each other to go on to greater heights; individuals sometimes lack the ability to motivate themselves in that way."

"I exercise better in a group than I can by myself because I get caught up in the enthusiasm of the group. The same thing happens to me when I am in a team environment at work."

"When everyone on a team pitches in, the job gets done a lot faster."

"I remember the ideas longer when I discuss them in the team meetings than if I were to read about the same ideas on my own."

"I know that when I have a chance to put my two cents into the discussion, I usually support the decision more than when I am simply told how things are going to be done."

"Teams help you look at things differently. Some team members listen to an idea or look at a problem and see it from a totally different angle from anyone else."

There certainly are some advantages to working individually, but we are more likely to make better decisions and even be motivated to work harder in a team environment.

However, we can realize the benefits of teaming and

take advantage of the strength that many bring to the team only if we are open to the ideas and perceptions of other team members. We must be curious, tolerant, and eager to see and hear life from the point of view of the others if we are to benefit from their intelligence and differing life experiences.

Most of us are open to the perception of others when they smell, taste, and touch the world differently than we do: Take note of the many different perfumes people prefer; the variety of Chinese, Mexican, and Italian restaurants that are the favorites of fellow workers; and the number of people in the same work area who complain of being too hot or too cold at the very same moment. We do smell, taste, and touch the world differently from those around us—and in most cases we are tolerant of the others' differences. Can we be as tolerant of team members who see and hear the world differently than we do? If we can, then we are opening our world to one of the greatest values of team interaction: the strength that comes from being receptive to diverse perceptions.

◇ Differing Perceptions and Tolerance ◇

In an effort to expose yourself to differing perceptions, ask at least five coworkers to examine the visual image that appears on page 18 and to tell you what they see. If all five get the same meaning from the image, then continue to expose people to the image until you have heard several different meanings. Take a few moments to discuss the meanings they perceive from the image compared to the meaning you perceive.[4] Now respond to these questions:

1. If there was a difference in perception between you and your coworkers, how would you characterize the way in which you and each coworker talked about it? _____

_____

_____

What image do you see in this figure?

	Yes	No
2. Did people try to insist that what they saw was the only meaning to be seen?	☐	☐
3. Was there a sense of curiosity about the meanings others received from the image?	☐	☐
4. Did you and your coworkers seem tolerant of the others' perceptions?	☐	☐
5. Did you get a sense that people were entitled to differing perceptions?	☐	☐

If you experienced tolerance, curiosity, and a genuine desire to understand the others' perceptions of what was viewed in the image, then we would encourage you to apply those characteristics when differing perceptions occur on a team. This same sense of tolerance, curiosity, and desire to understand is necessary for you to achieve the total benefits from working in a team environment.

   If these communication characteristics were lacking in your discussion of the image, we encourage you to strive for them. It might be easier to work toward this type of interaction if you all remember that meanings do not exist in images we view but in the people who view the images. The best we can hope to do is to understand others' meanings. This is critical to breaking the mold of individualism and working toward the dynamics of teaming.

◪ TEAMTHINK OR GROUPTHINK? ◪

We want your team experience to be beneficial to you as well as to your team. It is important for you to be aware of one crucial point in order to make the team experience work for you: Successful teams do not automatically happen. Working in a team can be a challenging process, and you and your team members must work hard to overcome the pitfalls. The following story illustrates this challenge that you may be facing:

> There once was a French scientist, named Jean-Henri Fabre. He had a very interesting passion in life—he studied caterpillars. At one point in his research, he conducted an experiment that involved processionary caterpillars—wormlike creatures that travel in long, unwavering lines, at the same pace and cadence.
>
> One day, Dr. Fabre placed a group of these wormy creatures onto the thin rim of a large flowerpot, forming a circle of caterpillars. In other words, the leader of the group of caterpillars was nose to tail with the last caterpillar in the slow, nonending procession. Even for Dr. Fabre, it was difficult to figure out who was the leader and which were the followers.
>
> During this entire day, Dr. Fabre watched the caterpillars go around and around in a circle without ever stopping. Later that night, he went home. The next

morning he arrived at his laboratory and guess what
he saw? He noticed that the caterpillars were still going
around in a circle. Then Dr. Fabre placed a supply of
food in the center of the flower pot. Even this did not
detour the caterpillars. Day after day, night after night,
the caterpillars paraded around and around. Do you
know when they finally stopped? Seven days later. Do
you know why? Because they started dying. They died
of starvation and exhaustion.[5]

Not for one moment did one caterpillar stop to look up,
eat some food, and try to stop the circle of travel. Instead
they just put their heads down and never looked up. Instead of thinking that maybe there was a better way, they
kept blindly following the caterpillar ahead of them until
they died.

Your challenge as a member of a team is to not act like
the caterpillars and blindly follow the members of your
team. Instead, maintain your own unique belief system
and viewpoint as you work on the team. We call this *teamthink*. If you give up your own uniqueness and way of looking at the world by not letting the group know your
position on topics, then your group could end up like Fabre's caterpillars. In other words, if all the members of your
group blindly follow each other, your group will go
around in circles, never make much progress, and never
perform well. We call this *groupthink*. This does not mean
that you should not try to cooperate with team members.
Rather, we mean that you should work together in an effective manner. In this case *effective* means that at times it is
fine to disagree and constructively discuss different views
so your team can develop the ideal way to approach a task
or problem.

Let's move from the sad plight of the caterpillars to a
different member of the animal kingdom, geese, to understand what we mean by working as a team while maintaining your own uniqueness:

1. Why do geese fly in a V formation? As each bird
flaps its wings, it creates an uplift for the following birds.

By flying in a V formation, the whole flock adds 71 percent greater flying range than if each bird flew alone.

Lesson for team members: Working together as a team can get you to where you want to go much faster and more efficiently. If team members share a common goal (direction) and work together as a unit, they can get to where they are going (achieve goals) more quickly and easily because they are traveling (working) on the thrust of one another and using the strengths of each other.

2. What happens to geese that try to fly alone? Whenever a goose falls out of formation, it suddenly feels the drag and resistance of trying to fly alone, and quickly gets back into formation to take advantage of the lifting power of the bird immediately in front.

Lesson for team members: Ignoring the group and going off on your own may not be a good idea. In order to achieve goals, team members should stay in sync in a mutual direction, and be willing to accept help and give help along the way.

3. Do geese ever get tired when they fly? When the lead goose gets tired, it rotates back into the formation, and another goose flies in the lead position.

Lesson for team members: As a member of a team, you have the luxury of working smarter, not harder, than if you were working alone. It can pay off to take turns doing the hard tasks and sharing responsibility and leadership with team members.

4. If geese work so well in a group, why do you always hear all that honking? Geese in formation honk from behind to encourage those up front to keep up their speed.

Lesson for team members: Successful teams have members who speak up and offer criticism when necessary to keep the group moving toward its goals. The key is to make sure the honking from team members is encouraging, not discouraging.

5. What happens to geese that can't keep up with the group? When a goose gets sick, wounded, or shot down, two geese drop out of formation and follow to help and protect it. They stay with it until it is able to fly again or dies. Then they attempt to catch up with the flock.

Lesson for team members: Successful teams have members who will stand by each other in difficult times and prosperous times.

We hope these lessons can help you prosper like geese within your group and help you and your team members avoid acting like caterpillars.

◪ BALANCING "ME" WITH "WE" ◪

A famous proverb states, "The best potential in 'me' is 'we.'" The message in this proverb is important to the success of your team. The crux of these words is that for you to reach your ultimate potential on the job, you need to work *with* your team, not against it. If a team member is focused on only himself and the credit he receives rather than focusing on the success of the team as a whole, his performance will suffer, and so will the whole team's. The following story illustrates this point and its connection to the success of your team:

> Two geese were about to start southward on their annual migration, when they were entreated by a frog to take him with them. The geese expressed their willingness to do so if a means of conveyance could be devised.
>
> The frog produced a long stalk of pond grass, and asked the geese to grab an end with their beaks. He clung to the middle of the grass by his mouth. In this way the three began their journey. Some farmers below noticed the strange sight. The men loudly expressed their admiration for the travel device and wondered who had been clever enough to discover it. Whereupon the vainglorious frog opened his mouth to say, "It was I," lost his grip, fell to the earth and was dashed to pieces.[6]

One moral to this story could be, "When you have a good thing going, keep your mouth shut," but we think there is a better one: "Team members who place too much emphasis on themselves and worry too much about who is going to get the credit will bring poor performance to themselves and their team." Conversely, team members who recognize that "the best potential in me is we" and understand that team success requires a total group effort will eventually achieve their individual goals and those of the team.

Realize that "the best potential in me is we" does not mean that team members should give up their individuality. Too much "we-ness" can lead to a situation where members act like caterpillars and blindly follow the team as a whole. The team may go around in circles, never make much progress, and never perform well. This type of groupthink is a common pitfall to team success.[7]

Here is an example of too much "we-ness" in a team. Have you ever been in a team situation where members were sitting around talking about a particular problem and in the course of that discussion, you had an important thought that went against the predominant view of most of the team? What did you do? Remain silent? Speak up? If you remained silent, you were helping your team experience groupthink or too much "we-ness." You were not maintaining your individuality, nor were you expressing your personal viewpoint. The outcome of your actions, especially if other members were also suppressing their divergent views, would likely be defective decision making and, consequently, poor team performance.

An effective team member in scenarios like the one above would not have remained silent. Effective teams must exhibit geeselike or teamthink behaviors as opposed to groupthink behaviors. Teamthink is a situation where team members strike a balance between themselves (the me) and the team (the we). This teamthink balance involves members' working together as a cohesive unit and constructively disagreeing when it is necessary. Additionally, members of teamthink teams encourage each member to express all of her views and ideas so that the optimal manner of performing a task or handling a problem can be determined.

The question that logically arises is, Where are you and your team at this moment? Is your team a groupthink team or a teamthink team? Are you striking a good balance between "me-ness" and "we-ness"? To help you answer these questions look at the corresponding characteristics of teams experiencing teamthink or groupthink:

Groupthink	*Teamthink*
■ Direct social pressure against differing views	■ Encouragement of differing views
■ Self-censorship of concerns	■ Open expression of concerns and ideas
■ Illusion of "we can't fail"	■ Awareness of limitations and threats
■ Illusion of unanimity	
■ Self-appointed mind guards that screen external information	■ Recognition of members' uniqueness
	■ Recognition of views outside the group
■ Collective efforts to rationalize	■ Discussion of collective group doubts
■ Stereotyped views of enemy leaders	■ Use of nonstereotypical views
■ Illusion of morality	■ Recognition of ethical and moral consequences of decisions

Take a moment to determine which type of symptoms your team is experiencing. If your team displays all teamthink symptoms and no groupthink characteristics, congratulations! You are unique in the world of teams because most teams during some point display groupthink-like symptoms. If your team does display some of these groupthink symptoms, don't panic. Keep reading; you'll find lots of guidance for overcoming obstacles—like groupthink—that impede your team's success.

◪ A WIN-WIN TEAM ATTITUDE ◪

"The greatest discovery of my time is that human beings can alter their lives by altering their attitudes." Think about this statement by William James for a moment. What does it suggest to you about you and your team? One interpretation is that our success in life is largely determined by our attitudes, over which we have substantial control.

Let's examine this a little further. A common definition for *attitude* is a "state of mind." What is your state of mind right now regarding your team? Is your attitude positive? Negative? The answer to this question is very important because, as James suggests, your attitude can have an impact on your life at home and at work. In terms of your work life, the nature of your attitude (positive or negative) toward your team can affect your individual success and happiness, as well as the overall success and happiness of your team. Those with a positive attitude can achieve great things; those with a negative attitude usually meet with mediocrity.

If you want to receive the maximum benefits from your team experience, you must develop a positive win-win attitude: a mind-set or way of thinking whereby a team member believes his participation in the team can benefit both himself and the team as a whole. There are no losers in this team game. Both the individual members and the team as a whole benefit from working together.

We do realize, however, that we all have bad days, and no one can be positive all of the time. The secret is to take control of your attitude so that you can experience positive win-win days most of the time. Following these tips can help keep your mind-set in a win-win attitude:[8]

1. Focus on the benefits of working on a team. Your team as a unit can accomplish more than you can individually; we call this *synergy*. Thus, focusing on what you can attain by working with your group can help you avoid any negative thinking about your team.

2. Seek the good in the people around you. Concentrate on the positive aspects of your team members. Although we realize that problems can result among team members, searching for the good in fellow members can help you overcome any interpersonal difficulties that could reduce the effectiveness of your team.

3. Seek the good in your workplace. Put some hard work into seeing the positive in your team since picking out the negatives doesn't usually require much effort. What are the potential career and social benefits from working with your team? What inspires you about working as a team? The more good you see, the more you can use it as a catalyst to make your team a success.

4. Learn to forgive. It's hard to maintain a positive attitude if you harbor resentments and grudges. Write down any anger or grudges you may have toward others, and then throw this list away. Maintaining a win-win attitude will be easier without the weight of the past resting on your shoulders.

5. Find humor in everyday occurrences. Research has shown that people who experience laughter in their lives are less prone to illnesses than those who laugh very little. Laughter can be a very helpful tool to the health of your team too. It can help you and your fellow team members keep a positive outlook. Learn to laugh at yourself and your team experiences rather than get angry about situations you can't change.

6. Let your positive attitude in one area spill over into another. If you find yourself thinking negatively about your team experiences, find an area in your life that is positive (e.g., friends, family, hobbies). You may discover that you can transfer some of these positive thoughts to your feelings about your team.

7. Talk positively with yourself and others. Talking positively with yourself can help you achieve a win-win attitude because you are what you think. If you tell yourself that you can work with your team to achieve great success for you and all your fellow team members, this thinking will increase the likelihood of that occurring. Also, find out what you can compliment and praise about a situation or person. Avoid constant complaining. Praise can lead to more effective team functioning.

8. Avoid attitude downers. *Attitude downers* are people who like to drag down your positive thinking. Remember that you are in control of your attitude. Protect your win-win attitude from negative lose-lose attitudes of others. Be strong, and your outlook will eventually spread to other team members.

9. Take control. It will be tough to have a good attitude if you just "allow" experiences to happen to you and your team. Take control of setting goals, and take responsibility for your decisions. Your attitude will benefit greatly because you and your team will know that you *created* your success; it was not due to chance or luck.

10. Stand up for what you believe. It's hard to have a positive attitude when you violate your own principles. We each have to live with ourselves twenty-four hours a day. Without personal ethics, these days can be quite unhappy. Stick to your beliefs regardless of the circumstances, and your attitude will continue to blossom.

11. Stop rushing. Do you find yourself rushing through your day because you feel you don't have enough time to complete all of your tasks? If your answer is yes, then your remedy for lack of time may be to run faster and rush rather than to work smarter. All this leads to is more stress for you. Just like biting your nails or overeating, rushing can become a habit rather than a response to a specific situation. You'll feel happier and more positive and still accomplish your goals if you speak and move more deliberately.

The Vision

Do you have a grand idea
To which some might laugh and smile?
They think it can't be done;
They call it a "someday I'll."

Then consider this story of two men;
Their business was selling shoes.
They were confronted with the same situation,
But each had differing views.

Both were sent to a far-away island
To test if their abilities were elite.
And they discovered, upon arrival,
The natives had nothing on their feet.

The first sadly called his boss
With a very large case of despair.
Relayed that there was no hope for business
Because everyone's feet were bare.

The second was filled with much elation;
Told his superior the good news.
Said he was going to make a million.
No one **yet** *was wearing shoes.*

The meaning in these few words
Is your thoughts can help you advance
Because what to some might spell disaster
Could be for you, your one big chance.

The secret to creating opportunities
Isn't money or political pull.
Simply, it's our attitude.
Is the glass half-empty or half-full?

A different real world example
Might help reveal this story's key.
It's a lesson of a pollinating insect,
The plight of the bumblebee.

According to the laws of science,
The bee should not be able to fly.
But this creature didn't acknowledge this
And instead gave flight a try.

So remember what history reveals
As you pinpoint your dreams with precision.
"That those who took the less traveled road
Were armed with nothing but their vision."
                                        —Christopher P. Neck

2

TEAM LEADERSHIP

The exercise of influence that facilitates, enables, and empowers others to constructively contribute their unique capabilities and knowledge to the team

What's Your Leadership Style?
Meeting the Challenge of Team Leadership
Can You Lead Others to Lead Themselves?
What Does a Team Leader Do?

◪ WHAT'S YOUR LEADERSHIP STYLE? ◪

You are the current leader of your work team, which has ten people on it. Dave, one of the members, has been a problem for your team recently. You were instrumental in his being hired a little over a year ago. You were impressed with his solid experience and especially the motivated attitude he seemed to display during his job interview. You still believe he has the intelligence and ability to be a solid performer.

Unfortunately, shortly after he began working on the team, his enthusiasm seemed to fade. For the past few weeks, he has been chronically late in completing his work, and you are concerned that his careless attitude is going to rub off on the others. He seems to feel put out every time you or other team members ask him to do something, and you have overheard him complaining on several occasions. You are convinced that his workload is not at all unreasonable and is in fact probably lighter than average. He just does not seem to be motivated and committed to his work and to the team.

You realize that Dave's behavior has to change, or he is going to become more of a problem than a help to you and the others. You have tried to give him time to adjust to his job, but several months have gone by, and things are getting worse instead of better.

You've decided that Dave requires some kind of special leadership attention from you, but you're not sure what.

Choose one of the three approaches listed below to deal with the situation, and write down a couple of ideas regarding how you would use the strategy to deal with Dave:

Approach 1: Be firm and directive with Dave. Use critical feedback and punishment to get him to change his behavior.

_____

_____

Approach 2: Develop an incentive plan. Use recognition and other rewards to improve his motivation.

_____

_____

_____

_____

Approach 3: Describe your vision for the team to Dave and your view of how you see him fitting into that vision as a means of obtaining his commitment.

_____

_____

_____

_____

Is there another approach you might use to provide leadership for Dave? If so, briefly describe it._____

_____

_____

_____

Interpretation

Approach 1 is direct and controlling. It means getting Dave to do what you want him to do whether he likes it or not and using your leadership authority to force or intimidate him to do it. This type of leadership is sometimes called the *Strongman* approach because it stems from the days of male-dominated leadership often based on intimidation and punishment.

Approach 2 focuses on an exchange relationship. Using the carrot (and sometimes the stick) in order to get followers to reach objectives is the key here. Again, it is not so important to this type of leader, sometimes called the *Transactor,* that others like what they are doing or believe in it. Instead, motivation is mostly based on providing rewards for doing what the leader wants.

Approach 3 is based on providing an inspiring vision. The

leader motivates others to pursue the cause spelled out in the leader's vision. The important aspect of this type of leadership is that followers believe in the leader and or the leader's cause. This type of leader can be called the *Visionary Hero.*

Each of the three choices can serve as a way to lead others. Unfortunately, all three center on the leader. The leader is in the limelight and tends to get all the credit; followers can feel as if they are pawns on a giant chessboard without really caring whether they do their best.

There is another alternative: *SuperLeadership.* It was designed specifically to fit with the challenges of leading empowered teams. The SuperLeader leads others to lead themselves. By serving as an example and encouraging and reinforcing followers for taking responsibility and initiative, as well as working effectively with their team members, the SuperLeader establishes the conditions so that the team and its members can mostly serve as their own leaders.[9]

Think about the idea of leading others to lead themselves in relation to this case. What ideas does SuperLeadership suggest for leading Dave?

Ponder what Lao-tzu wrote before you continue with your reading:

> *A leader is best*
> *When people barely know he exists,*
> *Not so good when people obey and acclaim him,*
> *worse when they despise him.*
> *But of a good leader, who talks little,*
> *When his work is done, his aim fulfilled,*
> *They will say:*
> *We did it ourselves.*

 MEETING THE CHALLENGE OF TEAM  LEADERSHIP

Picture yourself as a team leader.[10] Circle the letter next to the statement closest to your probable reaction to the situations listed below.

$$\Diamond \quad \Diamond \quad \Diamond$$

1. One of your team members changes a work procedure without your approval. The changes have created major delays, and management is upset. You have a meeting with the team member this afternoon. You will:

    a. Have him eliminate the changes and meet the deadline management wants.

    b. Discuss the deadline issue with him, and offer some incentive for adopting your approach and meeting the management goal.

    c. Explain the "big picture" rationale for the management concerns and your vision for how his work on this project will contribute to overall performance.

    d. Have the team member work up a plan for dealing with the delays, and address management's concerns. While indicating your support of your team member, you let him handle the situation.

2. Your team is getting busier, and your team members are overworked. A new member may be needed, but you're not sure about the definition of the new job. You will:

    a. Review the work structure of the team, evaluate whether a new person is needed, and if so design a job based on your estimation of the gaps and delays.

"Meeting the Challenge of Team Leadership" was coauthored with Maria Muto and Henry P. Sims, Jr.

    b. Call a team meeting and discuss the situation. Offer an increase in pay if the team can handle the increased productivity without adding another person.

    c. Call a meeting of your team and present your view of the situation and what a new person in the team should accomplish.

    d. Give the responsibility for analyzing the situation and, if necessary, developing the new job definition to the team. Make yourself available for suggestions and advice.

3. Your team operates as a largely independent sales and service unit, and sales have been dropping. Unless the market changes, you are afraid that you may have to lay off some of your team members. You will:

    a. Make the decisions for the layoffs based on the criteria you think are appropriate. You wait to inform the team of the layoffs until you are certain you will have to let some of them go.

    b. Call the team together, explain the situation, and offer incentives for members to work part time and thereby reduce the payroll burden.

    c. Call the team together, briefly explain the situation, and let them know about their importance in the overall success of the company.

    d. Call the team together, explain the situation, and work with them in solving the problem of lower sales. Work with them to address the needs of the situation.

Interpretation

If you answered:

Mostly a's. You are primarily a Strongman. You like to maintain control of the situation and make sure that followers comply with your directives.

Mostly b's. You are primarily a Transactor. You exchange incentives for compliance to get followers to act as you wish.

Mostly c's. You are primarily a Visionary Hero. You like to present your view of the big picture and inspire the others to commit to your vision.

Mostly d's. You are primarily a SuperLeader. You are working to develop and coordinate team members who are capable of leading themselves.

If leadership is viewed as a top-down process, and traditionally it has, this can create serious problems for both leaders and followers, especially in a team environment. It is no longer realistic to expect leaders to provide all the answers and direction. With the mounting competitive pressures from around the world, every employee's knowledge and ideas are critical. From the followers' perspective, having to deal with goals that they do not help shape and work methods that they do not help to develop leads to an understandable lack of motivation. Followers, like leaders, need to be acknowledged and appreciated as resources of significant value to their organizations. Followers are a critical factor in the survival of tomorrow's organization.

Consider and compare the four types of leadership summarized in Figure 1. SuperLeadership is designed to meet the challenges of leading empowered team members. The fundamental idea is to help team members become leaders in their own right. This means that the primary task of the team leader is to help team members master self-leadership skills. The SuperLeader facilitates this growth through strategies such as modeling self-leadership, encouraging and reinforcing team member self-leadership behaviors, allowing room for failure, and nurturing a work culture that supports initiative and individual responsibility.

Figure 1. Four approaches to leadership.

The Strongman	The Transactor	The Visionary Hero	The SuperLeader
• Focuses on command	• Focuses on rewards	• Focuses on visions	• Focuses on self-leaders
• Power stems from position and authority	• Power stems from reward and exchange	• Power stems from relationships and inspiration	• Power is shared
• Is the source of thinking and direction	• Is the source of thinking and direction	• Is the source of thinking and direction	• Thinking and direction come from both followers and leader
• Uses direction, command, assigned goals, intimidation, and reprimand	• Uses goal setting, rewards and punishment	• Uses communication of vision, emphasis on ideals, values, and inspirational persuasion	• Becomes a self-leader
• Followers comply based on fear	• Leads to self-serving minimal performance	• Leads to an emotional commitment based on the leader's vision	• Models self-leadership
• Followers become "yes men"	• Followers become "rational calculators"	• Followers become "inspired sheep"	• Encourages self-set goals
			• Creates positive thought patterns
			• Develops self-leadership through reward and constructive feedback
			• Promotes self-leading teams
			• Facilitates a self-leadership culture
			• Leads to commitment based on ownership
			• Team members become self-leaders

◢ CAN YOU LEAD OTHERS TO LEAD THEMSELVES? ◢

In today's rapidly changing and highly competitive business environment, effective leadership practice is critical to success. But what is effective leadership practice?

Some Common Views of Effective Leadership Practice

Leadership is typically viewed as a top-down process in which one person (a leader) influences another (a follower) to do what the leader wants done. This is often accomplished through threat and intimidation stemming from the leader's position of authority (the Strongman). At other times, a transactional approach is used in which the leader exchanges incentives for subordinate compliance with the leader's wishes (the Transactor). A more recent popular view of effective leaders suggests that they create and communicate inspiring visions that motivate others to do what the leader sees as desirable (the Visionary Hero).

Unfortunately, significant problems stem from these views of leadership and the kinds of behaviors they encourage us to act out when we find ourselves in positions of authority. No one person can have all the answers or even most of the answers. Even if it were realistic to expect persons in leadership positions to have the ability to provide the answers and directions and for followers simply to follow, we still would be faced with serious problems. Followers have a hard time getting excited about goals that they do not help shape and work methods that they do not help to develop. Followers, like leaders, want to feel they are competent and significant to their organization and that they are valued resources. The reality today is that if organizations are to survive, all employees must be valuable resources that share their knowledge and ideas, as well as their labor.

Stop and reflect for a moment. When you have served in positions of leadership, to what extent do you believe you kept the spotlight focused on yourself and away from your followers? Write your thoughts in the following space.

_____

_____

_____

From Leadership to SuperLeadership

SuperLeadership—leading others to lead themselves—is designed to meet the kinds of challenges team leaders face. According to SuperLeadership, an effective leader does not bend the wills of others to her own. Rather, she empowers others to stand on their own two feet and to feel ownership of their job. SuperLeadership suggests that the spotlight should be on followers at least as much as leaders. In fact, the fundamental idea is to help team members become leaders in their own right. This means that the leader's task becomes a process of helping others master self-leadership skills.[11] There are seven specific steps that you as a team leader can follow:

1. Become an effective self-leader. For example, set specific challenging but achievable goals and reward yourself for your own accomplishments. Redesign your own job so that you find it more motivating while still meeting your responsibilities. Practice thinking constructively and positively so that you take advantage of opportunities rather than retreat from obstacles.

2. Model self-leadership for team members. Once you've mastered some self-leadership strategies yourself, vividly display these effective techniques for your team members to learn from. Demonstrate self-leadership strategies in a clear and credible manner, and give team members a chance to try them out for themselves and to adapt them to their own needs.

3. Encourage team members to set their own goals.

Self–goal setting is so important that it deserves special attention. Help your team learn the importance of setting challenging but realistic targets for its performance. First, help team members set their goals; then gradually allow them to set goals for themselves.

4. Create positive thought patterns. Help team members to see their own potential and capabilities and believe in themselves. Also, encourage them to look for the opportunities nested in problems rather than focusing on all the reasons to give up and stop trying.

5. Reward self-leadership and promote constructive critical feedback. Recognize and reward team members for initiative, taking on responsibility, and using self-leadership strategies. The focus of praise should shift to effective self-leadership rather than just performance. Also, as team members become more confident, they will be better able to accept constructive critical feedback on how they can improve. The key is for the feedback to be constructive. Over time, team members should develop the ability to provide their own constructive feedback.

6. Promote self-leading teamwork. Encourage your team to work together and help one another. Teams are crucial for effective worker empowerment. Team members can encourage and reinforce one another.

7. Facilitate a self-leadership culture. Work to establish values and norms that center on initiative and self-leadership. If the first six steps are carried out effectively, this process should unfold naturally. In general, encourage, guide, and reward self-leadership behavior while continually demonstrating effective self-leadership in your own actions.

Take a moment to reflect again. Have you ever served as a SuperLeader for others: Your coworkers? Your children or other relatives? Write down your thoughts on how and when you did this.

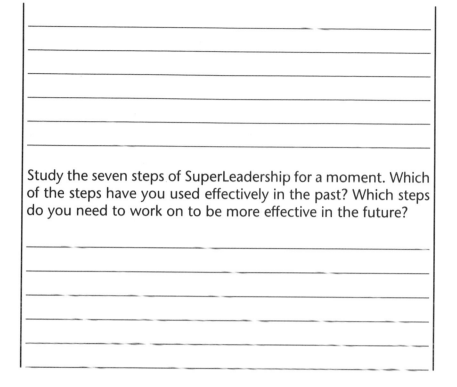

Study the seven steps of SuperLeadership for a moment. Which of the steps have you used effectively in the past? Which steps do you need to work on to be more effective in the future?

◢ WHAT DOES A TEAM LEADER DO? ◣

To understand your own views about team leadership, do the following exercise.

◇ Understanding Your Own Views on Team Leadership ◇

Imagine that you have recently been selected as an internal team leader on a team of twelve people. The persons in your team have an average of three years' experience in the company. The team itself has had a reputation of being fairly mediocre, consisting of average performers who are not committed to their work. Nevertheless, you believe they are fairly well trained and that they know what they are doing. Motivation seems to be the problem.

Your organization has been steadily moving to a more decentralized style of management. In the past year, the top executives have been talking more and more about the importance of employee involvement and participative management. Your own feeling is that the company does not really know what all this means but is reacting to pressure from growing competition in the industry and low workforce morale. With all the hype on participative management in the press, upper management seems to believe this is a direction the company has to go.

External team supervisors have been reduced significantly from a ratio of one per team two years ago to the current ratio of one coordinator (they are no longer called supervisors) for every six teams. Coordinators no longer directly supervise teams but instead provide advice and guidance when needed and see to it that teams have all the resources they need to do their work. Internal team leaders (your new position) are team members who provide day-to-day leadership within the team.

Your immediate challenge is to identify the distribution of responsibilities for you and your team. In establishing your preliminary plan, respond to each item in the following list, putting a 1, 2, or 3 in front of each item according to how you think that aspect of the team should be handled:

1 You decide or do on your own.

2 You receive input from the team and then decide or do on your own.

3 You participate as a team member with the rest of the team and then decide or do together.

Base your responses on how you expect the team to function once it is running the way you think it should. Assume that significant responsibility for each of the areas listed has been assigned to the team.

_____ Create team mission or vision

_____ Establish team goals

_____ Team planning

_____ Decide what work is done

_____ Decide who does each task

_____ Decide how each task is completed

_____ Decide when each task is completed

_____ Decide where each task is performed

_____ Conduct team member performance appraisals

_____ Decide on team member pay bonuses

_____ Provide training for team members

_____ Discipline team members

_____ Develop new team procedures

Interpretation

Count your 1s, 2s, and 3s. In general mostly 1s reflects more of a control style that fits with the traditional concept of boss. Mostly 2s suggests a middle-of-the-road approach with openness to participation but a belief that ultimately the leader should have the final word. Mostly 3s reflects a team focus based on a leadership style consistent with SuperLeadership—leading others to lead themselves.

When a team is getting established, more leadership influence (choosing 1s and 2s) can be helpful and even needed by the team. In the long run, however, teams tend to work better when they take more responsibility for themselves and learn to stand on their own without being overly dependent on a leader. This is a challenging lesson to learn for many team leaders. When the leader makes the decisions and solves the problems, short-run results may be fine, but the team does not learn to fend for itself. Effective team leaders learn the skill of facilitating teams to learn, gain confidence, and in general solve problems, make decisions, and lead themselves.

Team leaders can perform some helpful activities in many effective team-based organizations—for example:

1. Help the team to solve its own problems.
2. Make sure that the team has the resources and equipment it needs.
3. Arrange for useful training that enables the team to gain needed skills.

4. Facilitate team meetings at first, and then teach other team members to facilitate meetings.
5. Serve as a communication link for the team with management and other teams.
6. Be a good team member who works alongside other members.
7. Serve as an example of a supportive, fully contributing team member.

Holding On Means Letting Go

There was a very young girl
Attempting to fly her kite.
And as the wind grew stronger and stronger,
The child held on with all her might.

But instead of letting more string out,
She thought holding on was all she could do,
And in only just a few seconds,
The kite string broke in two.

The kid was quite perplexed
As a tear ran down her face.
The kite was hers no longer
As it drifted into space.

As I hope this example illustrates,
You must consider this to be the truth—
Gripping tighter might not be the answer;
Sometimes you have to let loose.

Whether it's a relationship or your child,
There is something you must know—
That in order to hold on,
Sometimes you have to let go.

—Christopher P. Neck

3

TEAM SELF-LEADERSHIP

Application of strategies that enable team members to provide themselves with self-direction and self-motivation, and ultimately to become effective, personally empowered contributors to their team

Preplay
Self-Talk
Managing Your Beliefs
Discovering Your Thinking Patterns
Self-Observation and Self-Evaluation
Self-Goal Setting
Self-Reward
What's Fun About Work?
Are You a Good Stress Manager?
Becoming a Master Self-Leader

▨ PREPLAY ▨

A mind not to be changed by place or time, the mind is its own place and in itself can make a heaven of hell, a hell of heaven.

—John Milton

Would you believe us if we told you there is a technique available to you that can help you and your team members perform better on the job? Would you believe us if we told you that this technique is available to you at no cost—not a single penny—and only a relatively minimal amount of your time? In fact, athletes have used this technique for years to help their performance. Golfers golf better, basketball players shoot better, and gymnasts tumble better because of it. The good news is that this technique is not only for people participating in sports. You too can benefit from it at work within your team.

This technique is a type of mental practice we call *preplay*. It means imagining the successful completion of an event before you actually do it. For example, consider a basketball player who, before a game, pictures himself making all of his free throws. By performing successfully in his mind, he should experience more confidence in the actual game situation and thus have a better chance at making his free throws.

Let's take another example, this one involving you and your team members. Assume that two of you begin working separately to complete similar challenging tasks. Suppose one of you pictures in your mind becoming very frustrated and nervous and eventually giving up on the project, in the process feeling humiliated in front of the other team members. This imagined experience could lead to lack of confidence and thus poor performance on the actual task. Suppose the other team member imagines a positive experience resulting in enormous praise from fellow team members. In this case, this team member would likely possess higher self-confidence before starting the actual project and probably enjoy this imagined success.

The point here is that your mind is a powerful tool,

and you can use it to achieve great success. Just as a hammer serves no benefit if you don't know how to use it correctly, the mental practice tool works only if you know how to use it correctly. Here are concrete steps to help you use this technique to improve your performance; practice these steps over and over, and you too can enjoy the benefits of preplay:

1. Close your eyes.

2. Relax, concentrate, and focus. Feel all the stress leaving your body. Beginning at your feet . . . feel all the stress leaving . . . move to your chest, then to the top of your head . . . feel all the stress leaving your body. Concentrate all of your energy on this mental practice exercise. Rid your mind of all distractions.

3. Focus on a specific challenging situation in which you would like preplay to help you perform well.

4. Talk positively to yourself. Tell yourself several times that you are confident and you have the power to perform well in this situation.

5. Now mentally picture yourself right before you are to begin this task (event, project, etc.).

6. Stay concentrated, relaxed, and focused.

7. Mentally rehearse successful performance of this challenging situation several times. See yourself in your mind as an active participant, not a passive observer. In other words, if you imagine shooting a basketball during a game, make sure you are standing on the court shooting rather than watching yourself from the stands.

8. Repeat Step 7.

9. Open your eyes. Smile. Praise yourself. You were successful in your mind. Now you should have a greater feeling of confidence that you will perform this event successfully in real life.

Here are a few more tips to ensure that preplay works for you:

1. Make sure you visualize your actions in normal motion as opposed to slow motion.
2. It may be helpful to picture a calming scene such as a beach, a mountain, a forest, or a pond, in trying to relax.
3. Repeat these steps over and over so that you gain preplay perfection. Repetition of mental practice is critical.
4. Space your practice sessions over a number of days rather than mentally practicing an event in one mass session.

◪ SELF-TALK ◪

"Puff, puff, chug, chug," went the Little Blue Engine. "I think I can—I think I can—I think I can—I think I can—I . . ."

Up, up, up. Faster and faster the little engine climbed, until at last they reached the top of the mountain.

And the Little Blue Engine smiled and seemed to say as she puffed steadily down the mountain, "I thought I could. I thought I could. I thought I could."[12]

As children, many of us heard or read these words. These same words—"I think I can, I think I can, I think I can"—can benefit you and your team members today! This well-known phrase is an example of a mental strategy known as *self-talk*—what you say to yourself. The way in which the Little Blue Engine talked to herself seemed to affect her performance (getting over the mountain). In the same way, we believe that self-talk can help you and your team members perform better on the tasks that you are responsible for completing and can help everyone get along better. In fact, if you are currently not doing well on your job or are having conflict with a fellow team member, it could possibly be related to what you are saying to yourself or what your team member is telling himself.

Now think for a moment. Have you ever told yourself any of the following?

"I don't have the talent."

"Joe [a team member] just doesn't like me."

"I hate working within a team."

"If only I was a little smarter, then I could do this job really well."

"If only I had more money."

"I'm too old to work that hard."

"Today just isn't my day."

If you are like most of us, you have told yourself negative things similar to these examples. They are negative in that they are *sappers*—types of self-talk that sap your energy, your self-confidence, and your happiness. Sappers are destructive self-talk; they prevent you from achieving your goals and feeling good about yourself and your team. Sappers do this because what you tell yourself every day usually ends up coming true. If you tell yourself you won't have a good day, you won't. If you tell yourself you can't lose weight, you won't. If you tell yourself that you don't enjoy working in a team, you won't. It is that simple.

You may be asking, "How do I change my self-talk so that I can get over my own personal mountain"? The following exercise can help change your sapper self-talk to self-talk that will help you and your team achieve more effective performance.

◇ Discovering Your Negative Self-Talk ◇

The exercise on page 51 has two parts. The first part asks you to remember seven past events and answer, What did you tell yourself at that time? Write your responses. Each question will require a significant amount of thought. Make sure you really try to relive the questions asked so that your answers are as accurate as possible.

In the second part of this exercise, identify any negative self-talk. Then right next to this, replace this negative self-talk with what you could have told yourself if you wanted your self-talk to be positive rather than sapping. We include two examples to help you.

Take a close look at your initial responses. Were there a lot of destructive sappers, or was your self-talk supportive and motivating? If the former is true, this is a signal to you that what you are telling yourself may be causing the negative events or emotions that you are experiencing within your team and at work in general. Notice that any negative self-talk is demotivating and negative and it seems to sap energy, happiness, and self-confidence.

Now look at the right-hand side of self-talk, and notice how positive, motivating, and supporting it is. Wouldn't you rather give yourself an advantage on the job by making your self-talk positive in the future? Of course, you would! Now that you are aware that your self-talk may be negative and you've practiced changing it to be positive, you are well on your way to improving your effectiveness.

Your goal is for positive self-talk to become a habit for you, so try to be aware of what you are telling yourself over the next several weeks. From the moment you get up in the morning until you go to sleep at night, remind yourself to talk positive. Repeat "Discovering Your Negative Self-Talk" exercise daily until you start to notice that you are having difficulty identifying any negative self-talk and that you have chased all the sappers away.

◤ MANAGING YOUR BELIEFS ◤

In 1954, a physical feat that was thought to be humanly impossible was achieved: Roger Banister ran the mile in four minutes. Since then, dozens of runners have accomplished this challenge, which had eluded others for so

(*Text continues on page 55.*)

"Managing Your Beliefs" is adapted from material in C. Manz, *Mastering Self-Leadership* (Englewood Cliffs, NJ: Prentice Hall, 1992).

Negative Self-Talk	Positive Self-Talk
"I hate working within a team."	"While this is a new experience for me, I know that if we all make a good effort toward cooperating, we will make a much better product than if we were working by ourselves. And it will be fun getting to know each other."
"I'll never lose this extra weight."	"I will lose this weight. It will take a lot of determination and willpower. I will achieve my goal of losing one pound a week."

Part One

What Did You Tell Yourself at That Time?

Part Two

Positively Rephrase Negative Self-Talk

1. Recall a project or activity that you have begun or considered beginning.

_____ _____

_____ _____

_____ _____

2. Think of a time that you were feeling very lonely.

3. Think of a day that you were feeling very stressed and overwhelmed at work.

4. Recall criticism you may have received from a team member.

5. Think of a recent compliment that a team member gave you.

6. Think of a day when you were feeling negative about yourself.

7. Think of a day where you were experiencing some physical symptoms such as a headache or achy muscles.

long. Banister later expressed the view that a new mental outlook for runners was responsible for those accomplishments, not improvements in running equipment or techniques. Once people *believed* it was possible to run a mile in less than four minutes, a major barrier to its accomplishment was removed—and then they actually did it! This idea that what we can conceive of or believe is possible and can be achieved is not new.

One perspective for dealing with your personal behavior and emotional reactions in an attempt to improve them involves focusing on your beliefs. The argument is that your beliefs, rational and irrational, determine your reactions to events—and ultimately to the quality of your life experiences. Any irrational fears or hang-ups you possess can be traced to irrational beliefs. In other words, it is not the external event that causes your reaction to it but your beliefs about that event. According to this view, by recognizing, confronting, and altering those beliefs, you can improve your behavior and mental outlook.

Imagine that you have a strong fear of speaking in front of groups, including your team, but you desperately want to overcome this difficulty and become a competent and confident public speaker. One way of dealing with your fear is to try to discover and change the beliefs that cause it. Perhaps you worry that people will think less of you if you do not express yourself articulately, or that others know more than you do and you would display your ignorance by speaking. More constructive alternative beliefs can help you overcome the fear. For example, when you are among friends, you use an informal, imperfect style of speaking, and this style is not likely to cause them to devalue your friendship. And in both work and personal situations, there are sure to be subjects on which you would be the expert in the group.

Once you identify your beliefs, examine them; if they are irrational, your goal is to eliminate or replace them with ones that are more constructive. Examining the beliefs you hold and then dealing with those that are hindering your self-leadership may well increase your personal effectiveness. The importance of managing your beliefs is illustrated in the following story:

> A young girl was depressed because she was not beautiful. She was discouraged, but as she grew older, her attitude changed. "I realized that not being beautiful was actually a blessing in disguise," she said. "It forced me to develop inner resources and strength. I came to understand that women who can't lean on their beauty must work harder to have the advantage." [13]

This woman realized her belief that "outward appearance was the only important type of beauty" was irrational, so she got rid of it. And guess what eventually happened to her? Golda Meir went on to become the first woman prime minister of Israel.

Read over the following for guiding your attempts at examining and improving your beliefs. Then complete the following short exercise to help you get started in making improvements.

Analyzing and Improving Your Beliefs

1. Identify the types of tasks and activities for which your beliefs are especially important—that is, where your beliefs have a significant impact on your actions and feelings.
2. How accurate do you think these beliefs are?
3. Do these beliefs affect your actions and feelings positively or negatively?
4. Identify your inaccurate or dysfunctional beliefs. Can you think of at least one reason to challenge each of these beliefs?
5. Identify more positive and useful beliefs to take their place.

◇ Improving Your Belief System ◇

1. Think of some challenging problems or tasks where your beliefs and judgments were very important. Identify several

occasions when your results were unsatisfactory. Write down these occasions and results._____ _____

_____

_____

_____

_____

2. Describe how your beliefs affected your actions and reactions in the situations you listed (for example, did your beliefs affect your chosen course of action positively or negatively?)._____ _____

_____

_____

_____

_____

3. Were your beliefs accurate in those situations? (Of course, hindsight always seems to be perfect, but try to search rationally for patterns in your beliefs on those occasions that were dysfunctional as well as for those that were constructive.)

4. Identify some useful, constructive beliefs that you might have substituted for your dysfunctional ones on those occasions you have noted. _____ _____

_____

_____

_____

_____

5. How might your actions have changed if they had been based on these alternative beliefs?_____

_____

_____

_____

6. How might your results have changed?_____

_____

_____

_____

_____

Another simple exercise is to analyze and manage your beliefs to help you through difficult situations you face now.

◇ How Can You Respond Better? ◇

Do you find yourself reacting destructively to difficult situations, such as an argument with a coworker or spouse? List a few of these typical situations. For each, identify the beliefs or assumptions that underlie your reactions. Then list alternative, more constructive beliefs or assumptions.

*Situation:*_____

_____

_____

*Your beliefs or assumptions:*_____

_____

_____

*More constructive beliefs or assumptions:*_____

_____

_____

*Situation:*_____

_____

_____

*Your beliefs or assumptions:*_____

_____

_____

*More constructive beliefs or assumptions:*_____

_____

_____

*Situation:*_____

_____

_____

*Your beliefs or assumptions:*_____

_____

_____

*More constructive beliefs or assumptions:*_____

_____

_____

◪ DISCOVERING YOUR THINKING ◪ PATTERNS

For each pair of statements, circle the letter of the statement that better represents what you honestly think. If you agree with both statements, choose the one you agree with more.

1. **a.** There is a real opportunity built into every problem.

   b. Anything that can go wrong will.

2. **a.** A bird in the hand is worth two in a bush.

   b. Real opportunities are worth sticking your neck out for.

3. **a.** Most people cannot be counted on.

   b. Every person is a valuable resource in some way.

"Discovering Your Thinking Patterns" is adapted from C. Manz, *Mastering Self-Leadership* (Englewood Cliffs, N.J.: Prentice Hall, 1992).

4. **a.** Difficulties make us grow.

   b. Difficulties beat us down.

5. **a.** The world is full of impossibilities.

   b. Anything that we can conceive of is possible.

6. **a.** When half of the days in an enjoyable vacation have passed, I still have half of my vacation to enjoy.

   b. When half of the days in an enjoyable vacation have passed, my vacation is half over.

7. **a.** The best approach to dealing with energy shortages is conservation.

   b. The best approach to dealing with energy shortages is to develop new energy sources.

8. **a.** Life after death.

   b. Death after life.

9. **a.** Failure is an opportunity to learn.

   b. Failure is a negative outcome to effort.

10. **a.** Happiness is the absence of problems.

    b. Problems are the spice of life.

Scoring

For each of the ten items, circle the letter in the column below that corresponds to the choice you made for that item. Then count the number of letters circled in each column (I and II), and figure the total at the bottom of the columns.

	I	II
1.	a	b
2.	b	a
3.	b	a
4.	a	b
5.	b	a
6.	a	b
7.	b	a
8.	a	b
9.	a	b
10.	b	a
Total	_____	_____
	Opportunity Thinking	Obstacle Thinking

Interpretation

If your Column I total was higher than Column II, your thinking patterns tend to reflect opportunity thinking more than obstacle thinking. The reverse is true if your Column II total was higher than Column I. The greater the difference is between the two totals, the more you tend toward one pattern or the other. In general, a higher score on opportunity thinking reflects some desirable self-leadership tendencies; a higher score for obstacle thinking may indicate some fundamental problems.

Of course, interpret your results on this exercise cautiously. The way you score may reflect your current mood or outlook as opposed to any long-term tendencies. On the other hand, an exercise such as this is useful in helping you to reflect on the pattern of thinking that you tend to adopt in examining and approaching different situations.

Opportunity Thinking vs. Obstacle Thinking

There are two types of thought patterns that can be adopted: *opportunity thinking* and *obstacle thinking*. Opportunity thinking involves a pattern of thoughts that focus on the opportunities and possibilities inherent in situations or challenges. Creative, innovative individuals who contribute to the major breakthroughs and advances in our world usually possess this pattern of thinking. Their beliefs, their imagined future experiences, and their self-talk spur them to undertake new opportunities. An obstacle thinking pattern, on the other hand, fosters avoidance of challenges in favor of more secure actions, often with less substantial potential payoffs.

To illustrate opportunity versus obstacle thinking, consider this story from the life of Thomas Edison:

> Edison's laboratory was virtually destroyed by a fire in December 1914, and the buildings were insured for only a fraction of the money that it would cost to rebuild them. At the age of sixty-seven, most of Edison's life's work went up in flames on that December night.
>
> The next morning, Edison looked at the ruins and said, "There is a great value in disaster. All our mistakes are burned up. Thank God we can start anew." Three weeks after the fire, Edison delivered his first phonograph.[14]

Edison definitely was an opportunity thinker here—that is, he viewed the fire as a chance for a fresh start rather than as an excuse to quit. The question for you is, How do you view "fires" or problems with your team: as obstacles or as opportunities?

All of us can possess both of these types of thought patterns at different times and in different situations. There are undertakings that pose too much personal risk and should be avoided. On the other hand, we often find ourselves caught up in difficult situations unexpectedly. Avoiding the situation is no longer a choice; the issue now becomes one of how to deal with it.

We probably tend to rely on certain thought patterns more than others in dealing with life's challenges. For example, you might think that you should seek out worthwhile challenges because they will help you to grow. Or your thoughts might be that you should try to avoid new situations because they could cause possible problems. You might think that the world is unfair, or your thoughts could be that the world is basically good and that honest effort is rewarded.

Remember that the pattern your thinking takes can influence your actions, your satisfaction with life, and your personal effectiveness. Working to develop a habit of opportunity thinking usually leads to better results over the long run. Too much obstacle thinking can get anyone in a rut of avoiding challenges, innovation, and personal growth as an individual and a team member. This is why making an effort to manage your beliefs and self-talk and using other mental strategies such as preplay are so important.

◢ SELF-OBSERVATION AND ◢ SELF-EVALUATION

The cement that lays the foundation for your self-leadership as a team member is the information you possess about yourself—in other words, your self-awareness. By observing your own behavior and its causes (for example, why you behave in desirable or undesirable ways), you are provided with the necessary information to manage yourself more effectively.

Self-observation and evaluation involves determining when, why, and under what conditions you use certain behaviors. For example you might think, "That is the third time I've lost my temper and criticized someone today, and I've done it several other times this week. I wonder what's wrong and why I'm behaving like such an ogre." Or if you feel you are not accomplishing enough each day at work because of wasted time, you can study the distractions that

---

"Self-Observation and Self-Evaluation" is adapted from material in C. Manz, *Mastering Self-Leadership* (Englewood Cliffs, NJ: Prentice Hall, 1992).

lure you. Perhaps you are spending too much time en-
gaged in informal conversations. By observing the amount
of informal talking you participate in and the conditions
that exist at the time, you can learn more about this behavior. If you spend five hours chatting during the eight-hour
workday, you probably have a problem. And if you recognize that most of these conversations begin during a visit
to the water cooler, you have useful information to help
you cut down on that behavior.

If you record your self-observations, you add power
to this strategy. A handy pen and a note card may be all
you need to make brief notes to examine in detail later.

Self-observation can provide the foundation for evaluating and managing all team member behavior. Several
other distinct strategies build on this foundation. It is important to remember that you already use these strategies
in your daily living; the problem is that you often use them
unknowingly and ineffectively.

Look over this checklist summarizing the major steps
for practicing self-observation and evaluation. It will guide
you in completing the self-observation exercise on page 65.

Checklist for Self-Observation and Evaluation

☐ Use self-observation as a basis for self-leadership.

☐ Identify the team member behaviors you feel are especially important that you would like to increase or reduce in yourself. Pick one that you would like to begin
to work on in "Understanding Your Behavior Through
Self-Observation," the exercise that follows.

☐ Keep a record about the behavior on a small card or
piece of paper. Try to make these notes soon after the
behavior happens.

☐ Write down the date and time when the behavior
occurs.

☐ Note the conditions that exist when the behavior is dis-

◇ Understanding Your Behavior Through Self-Observation ◇

Intentionally observe yourself for the next week. Make notes about a behavior that you want to monitor on a small note card. Keep it handy. Include the date and time, what was happening, and why you think the behavior occurred. Make these notes soon after the behavior happens.

Behavior I want to observe this week: _____

_____

Date	Time	What was happening?	Why do I think it happened?

After trying this method for a week, ask yourself, "Was I successful in gaining a better understanding of this behavior?" If not, can you think of another way to help yourself keep track of the behavior you want to change?

played (e.g., Where were you standing or sitting? What were you doing just before the behavior occurred?).

☐ Identify other important factors concerning this behavior (e.g., who was present at the time or how you were feeling).

☐ Note any insights you had as to why you think the behavior happened.

An important part of this self-observation exercise is to become more aware of when you are engaging in the behavior you want to change. As you become more self-aware when the behavior occurs, it will be easier to stop and take time to write down your thoughts about its occurrence. Try to keep the process simple enough so that you will not be discouraged from using it.

After you have observed yourself and your use of this behavior over time, evaluate your progress. You will be better prepared to take action by setting specific goals to help change the behavior and its effect on your team.

◤ SELF-GOAL SETTING ◥

"I don't know where I'm going, but I'm getting there awfully fast," gasped the man as he scurried on past.

It is futile to exert effort with no direction. One way you can direct your efforts as a team member is through the use of personal goals. What you strive toward in terms of long-term life achievements as well as on a daily basis influences your behavior. Often we are not clear on what our goals really are. You may wish to become a highly effective team member, for example, but do not settle on how to go about becoming one or even what an effective team member

"Self-Goal Setting" is adapted from C. Manz, *Mastering Self-Leadership* (Englewood Cliffs, NJ: Prentice Hall, 1992).

is. The systematic, thought-out, intentional setting of personal goals can influence behavior in positive ways.

Self-set goals need to address your long-range pursuits and short-run objectives. If you decide on a long-range goal of becoming a top performer and reaching the highest skill level of employees in your company, you need to accomplish many short-range goals to get there. For example, you can work to accomplish a short-term goal of mastering a specific task or successfully completing a useful training program. The immediate behavior could be focused on learning one step of the task you want to master. The shorter-range goals should be consistent with the longer-range goals for maximum effectiveness. You must first engage in the necessary self-analysis for understanding what you ultimately want to accomplish before you can set the goals that must be reached in order to achieve those ends. This takes effort. Also, your goals are likely to change over time. Nevertheless, it is important that you try to have current goals for your immediate efforts.

Generally goals are more effective for managing immediate behavior if they are specific and challenging yet achievable. If you set unreasonable goals that you cannot realistically achieve, you are likely to do more harm than good. Realistic goals, on the other hand, can be very satisfying when you achieve them.

If you understand what makes a team member effective and what you want to accomplish, then you can set specific, achievable goals, such as learning one new part of a specific task. It is often helpful to record both long-term and immediate goals and then modify them as necessary. We all spend a great deal of time doing things on our teams. A little effort expended on setting self-goals can help us to have purpose and direction so that our efforts are not wasted.

The man stopped abruptly with surprise and in a panting voice said, "Why, I'm right where I started. I've gotten nowhere."

Use self–goal setting to establish direction for your efforts. Look over the checklist; then complete the exercise that follows, "Setting Your Self-Goals."

Checklist for Self-Goal Setting

☐   Conduct a self-analysis to help you establish long-term goals.

☐   Establish long-term goals for your work and life (e.g., what kind of team member would you like to be a year from now?).

☐   Establish short-term goals for your immediate efforts.

☐   Keep your goals specific and concrete.

☐   Make your goals challenging but reasonable for your own abilities.

☐   When feasible, let other team members know about your goals so they can help provide you with support and incentives to achieve them.

◇ Setting Your Self-Goals ◇

Answer the following questions to help you set long-term and short-term goals.

Long-Term Goals

1. What do I value most as a team member (e.g., high performance, big pay bonuses, acceptance by other team members)? _____

_____

_____

2. What would I most like to accomplish as a team member? What are my long-term goals? (An interesting way to approach this question is to write your obituary the way you would want your team to describe you if they were asked to write it. Include all that you would like to have accomplished as a team member.) _____

_____

_____

Goals for Developing My Abilities

3. What are my primary strengths and weaknesses that are related to what I would like to accomplish as a team member? _____

_____

_____

_____

_____

4. What do I need to do to prepare myself to accomplish my long-term team member goals (e.g., education, skills that need developing)? _____

_____

_____

_____

Short-Term Goals

5. What do I need to do now to progress toward my long-term goals (e.g., learn how to perform a new team task, read a book related to my work on the team)? _____

_____

_____

6. My short-term goals are (update these as needed): _____

_____

_____

◢ SELF-REWARD ◣

One of the most powerful methods for leading yourself to be a good empowered team member is self-reward. You can influence your actions positively by rewarding yourself for desired behavior. Furthermore, you are capable of rewarding yourself at both a physical and a mental level.

At the physical level, reward yourself with things you desire—perhaps a nice dinner or even just a hot cup of coffee after completing an important team task. By rewarding yourself with these desired items, you can positively affect your future work activity. The important point is to reward yourself with things that you enjoy when you accomplish desired objectives. Many of us do this without realizing it is happening. To increase your own motivation and effectiveness, the challenge is to identify those things you find rewarding and then use them intentionally to reward your behavior.

You can also reward yourself at a mental level through self-talk and using your imagination. If a team member finally solves a stubborn problem the team has been fighting about, she may appear calm on the outside, but if we could listen inside her head we might hear, "Ya hoo! I did it! I'm a genius! I'm the best! Ya hoo!"

We all engage in self-rewarding self-talk after big successes like these, but why not try to use this powerful method for less momentous occasions? In fact, we all probably could improve our own behavior significantly if we purposefully sought out our desired behaviors and gave ourselves an internal word of praise when we found ourselves using those behaviors.

This kind of praise would be especially helpful for team members who are quick to criticize themselves. We all have a choice between focusing on what we have done right, and building ourselves up, or focusing on what we

"Self-Reward" is adapted from C. Manz, *Mastering Self-Leadership* (Englewood Cliffs, NJ: Prentice Hall, 1992).

have done wrong, and getting down on ourselves. Research in this area indicates that the former strategy is the more effective one. Guilt and self-criticism may have their place in keeping you from engaging in undesired acts, but to rely on these and ignore self-praise is a poor way to lead yourself. Your self-esteem, enthusiasm, and enjoyment in life would likely suffer.

You can also reward yourself in your imagination. For example, you can journey to your favorite vacation spot in an instant through your imagination. Close your eyes and see the deep blue waters and the white sand beaches with seagulls overhead, and feel the warm sun on your face. Or maybe it's the brisk, cold air you feel rushing across your face as your skis glide gracefully through the new-fallen snow. Wherever and whatever that place is, you can go there in an instant. You can take the trip as a reward for finally getting that difficult report done or for accomplishing some other task. You might even hang a picture of that place on a wall and keep souvenirs nearby to help you make that mental trip whenever you choose.

You can combine the physical and mental levels to exercise a particularly powerful self-reward strategy: Take short, imaginary trips as you accomplish your tasks throughout the year and then physically enjoy that same vacation after the months of hard work. In this way, you reward both your short-term and long-term activities.

Use your imagination to reward yourself in countless other ways. Picture the success and esteem you will experience and enjoy when your team receives recognition and you get that team bonus you are working toward. Enjoying such an image after completion of each difficult task could help you to maintain the motivation you need as you face your labors. The mind is capable of being a powerfully motivating tool. If you are to become a truly effective team member, you need to master the use of this tool. In doing so, you can make the effort you expend seem worthwhile, if not truly enjoyable.

To help you achieve self-motivation through self-reward, use this checklist. After you read it, do the exercise that follows.

Checklist for Self-Reward

☐ Identify the objects, thoughts, and images that motivate you.

☐ Identify your most desired team behaviors and activities.

☐ Reward yourself when you successfully complete a team activity or engage in a desired behavior with a desired physical object, enjoyable or praising thoughts, or pleasant images.

☐ Develop the habit of being self-praising and self-rewarding for your accomplishments.

◇ Learning How to Use Self-Reward ◇

1. What physical objects or events do you find rewarding (e.g., a cup of coffee, a delicious dinner, an evening out)?_____

_____

_____

_____

2. What thoughts or images do you find rewarding (e.g., self-praising thoughts, imagining your favorite vacation spot, thoughts about future career success and prestige)?_____

_____

_____

3. Identify team behaviors that you would like to increase or improve on that require special motivation for you to do them (e.g., working on a difficult project, reading a technical book)._____

_____

_____

Try rewarding yourself for working on the team activities you just identified with both physical and mental rewards. Keep track of your efforts on these behaviors, the rewards you use, and the results and ideas for future improvement stemming from the self-reward process (such as the discovery of more effective rewards). Keep a record such as the one shown in the Self-Reward Record on page 74.

◤ WHAT'S FUN ABOUT WORK? ◤

The blizzard hit the forest with a tremendous force, leaving a deep layer of new-fallen snow. The beaver was in a bad mood as he struggled toward the river. The snow made it hard to move, and he was very irritated as he trudged along. Then the beaver noticed the whistling of the otter who was playfully sliding and rolling over slopes on his way to the river. "Why are you whistling on this horrible day?" snapped the beaver, obviously out of sorts. "Why, it's a great day," the otter sang out, "the best day I've had since yesterday, which was great too." The beaver sneered at this response and continued to complain as he trudged forward. The otter continued to slide and roll along playfully, whistling while he went. They both reached the river.

One powerful strategy for exercising self-leadership is to make work more fun by identifying aspects of it that you naturally enjoy and building in those features as often as possible. For example, a team meeting can be held in a pleasant location. The same issues discussed in a formal conference room will seem very different when they are addressed in an informal setting, even outdoors. Similarly, a person who enjoys eating out can enjoy communicating a message face to face with a team member over lunch rather than during a formal team meeting. Thus, one of

---

"What's Fun About Work" is adapted from material in C. Manz, *Mastering Self-Leadership* (Englewood Cliffs, NJ: Prentice Hall, 1992).

◇ My Self-Reward Record ◇

Behavior	Reward Used	Results

the more obvious ways to make activities more naturally enjoyable is to choose a pleasant context for the task, which is in essence part of the task.

Also, we can usually identify several ways of accomplishing many of our activities. By choosing to accomplish these tasks in more enjoyable ways, we are building in natural rewards for our efforts. This involves searching for features of your activities that provide you with feelings of competence (that you are capable and perform well), self-control (that you have significant control over what you do and how you do it), and purpose (that your work has value and meaning and serves a useful purpose). Evidence has shown that these three elements can make a task more naturally rewarding. Your work and life in general can be more fun if you take them seriously enough to play at them and make them more enjoyable.

Making your work more enjoyable can provide benefits beyond you and your team's work success. Did you know that when you can say, "I love my work," you reduce your risk of heart disease? Indeed, a study completed by the Massachusetts HEW Department explored the cause of heart disease. Participants were asked two questions: "Are you happy?" and "Do you love your work?" The results suggest that those who answered yes have a better chance of not getting heart disease.[15] Building natural rewards into your job to make it more enjoyable may benefit you and your team's health and performance.

Build in natural rewards, and do worthwhile things that you naturally like whenever possible. Self-management strategies can help you overcome your formidable obstacles when they arise, but when there is a choice, use the power of natural rewards. You can be successful and create a better world in the process if your work is inspired.

Checklist for Building Natural Rewards Into Your Activities

Read over the following checklist; then do the exercise.

- ☐ Think about your current tasks and where and how you do them.
- ☐ Identify pleasant contexts (locations, situations, conditions) in which you could perform your activities so that they would be more pleasant and naturally rewarding or find ways of making your current work surroundings more pleasant.
- ☐ Identify activities that could be built into your job, such as a different way of accomplishing a task that would make your job naturally rewarding.
- ☐ Redesign your job to allow you to work in the contexts and to incorporate the activities that will make your job more naturally enjoyable.

◇ **Learning How to Build Natural Rewards** ◇
Into Your Activities

Give some thought to each of the items below; then write your responses.

1. List some tasks that you need to complete that you do not particularly enjoy doing.

_____

_____

_____

_____

_____

2. Identify different, more pleasant contexts in which you could perform these tasks or ways of making your current work environment more pleasant.

_____

_____

_____

_____

_____

3. Identify activities that you find naturally rewarding (provide you with a sense of competence, self-control, and purpose) that could be built into your tasks.

_____

_____

_____

_____

4. Redesign your tasks. Use your ideas from items 2 and 3 as a basis for redesigning some of your tasks. Specify plans for redesigning tasks, including contexts and activities that could make your work more naturally rewarding.

_____

_____

_____

_____

◢ ARE YOU A GOOD STRESS MANAGER? ◢

You probably have heard the word *stress* mentioned numerous times. Stress is the wear and tear on your body due to your response to events in your life at work, play, and home. These responses are based on an inability or perception that you are unable to take control of your life.

Are you experiencing stress right now in your life? Is it the result of events occurring within your team? Do you feel overwhelmed, maybe even paralyzed, by this stress that you are feeling? Do you feel you have no control over

the events causing you stress? To help you answer these
questions, first complete the following quiz.[16]

◇ Are You a Good Stress Manager? ◇

Rate each item **1** (almost never), **2** (sometimes), **3** (frequently),
or **4** (almost always).

Rating

1. I worry I won't find another job if I lose this one.   _____

2. I wake up worrying about my work.   _____

3. I'm upset about the increased demands at work.   _____

4. I find myself getting irritable or angry.   _____

5. I speed impatiently from one task to another.   _____

6. I don't have enough control over how I do my
work.   _____

7. I don't feel appreciated at work.   _____

8. I worry about whether I can keep up at work.   _____

9. I wonder whether I'm really doing a good
enough job.   _____

10. It seems that nobody wants to know what I'm
feeling.   _____

11. I have trouble knowing what I'm really feeling.   _____

12. I hold in my feelings until they finally erupt.   _____

13. It's hard to make enough time for friends and
family.   _____

14. People close to me complain that I'm not available enough.   _____

15. I'm too worn out to give much time to my relationships.   _____

Total Points   _____

Interpretation

Less than 25: You're managing stress well.

25–34: You could be in for some emotional and physical discomfort.

35–44: The chances are high that stress could be creating a great deal of emotional and physical pain in your life.

Over 45: Experts suggest you probably should consult a physician and a career counselor as well.

If your results from the quiz suggest you are experiencing stress, you are not alone. The United States Clearing House for Mental Health Information estimates that American industry experiences a loss in productive capacity of more than $17 billion annually because of stress-induced mental dysfunction.

The good news is that there are strategies to help you take control of your life and manage the stress that you are experiencing. If you practice the following strategies, you should be able to break the chains of stress that are holding you back from reaching your higher potential. Once you master these, you can teach your fellow team members these skills to manage their own stress.

1. **Take hold of the wheel.** Believe that you are in control of your life. You must truly internalize the words of a famous poet, William Ernest Henley, "I am the master of my fate, I am the captain of my soul." Take charge of your life at this moment. Grab hold of the wheel now!

2. **You are what you think.** A large part of the stress you are experiencing may be due to the way you are thinking about events in your life. Research shows that those who view challenges in their lives as opportunities to grow rather than obstacles toward failure are more successful and happier people. Are you an opportunity or an obstacle thinker?

3. **Don't worry, be happy.** Do you tend to worry?

Worry prevents you from being able to work effectively. Most of the things you are worrying about will never happen, so stop worrying about things that probably won't happen. Worrying only creates stress and wastes your energy.

4. Time is precious; don't waste it! Do you frequently think, "If I only had more hours in the day, then I could get accomplished what I need accomplished"? Effective time management may be the answer to reducing your stress. Use those techniques to help chase your stress away.

5. Listen to yourself. Your behavior, feelings, and level of stress may be due to the daily conversations that you have with yourself. In other words, your self-talk may be the cause of the stress that you are experiencing. Stop and listen to what you are telling yourself about a difficult situation or a problem with a team member. Are you telling yourself positive or negative things? If the record player inside you is constantly playing negative songs, this is probably a major source of your stress. The solution is to change records and start talking positively to yourself.

6. Put up positive pictures on the walls of your mind. Perform mental imagery—preplay—before an activity that is stressful to you. Mentally picture yourself successfully performing a task before you actually have to complete it. This should help reduce your fear, worry, or anxiety about an upcoming activity at work.

7. Give your body a tune-up. The last stress buster is to take care of your body. Practice these three Es:

- Easy does it. Take time to relax.
- Exercise. Physical exercise rejuvenates your mind and body.
- Eat smart. Proper nutrition can build your energy supply. Eat a balanced diet.

To see if you are *creating* stressful thinking answer the following questions.[17] Then complete the exercise.

◇ ◇ ◇

	Yes	No

1. **All-or-nothing thinking.** You see things as black or white (e.g., if total perfection is not achieved, then you think you've completely failed). ☐ ☐

2. **Overgeneralization.** You generalize a specific failure or a negative result is generalized as an endless pattern. ☐ ☐

3. **Mental filter.** You dwell on single negative detail, which distorts all other aspects of your perception of reality. ☐ ☐

4. **Disqualifying the positive.** Even if you experience something positive, you mentally disqualify it from having any relevance or importance. ☐ ☐

5. **Jumping to conclusions.** You draw negative conclusions regarding situations despite a lack of concrete evidence to support these conclusions. ☐ ☐

6. **Magnifying and minimizing.** You exaggerate the importance of negative factors and minimize the importance of positive factors related to your situation. ☐ ☐

7. **Emotional reasoning.** You interpret reality based on the negative emotions you experience. ☐ ☐

8. **"Should" statements.** You use statements in your self-talk such as "should" and "shouldn't" and "ought" and "must" to coerce or manipulate yourself into taking actions. ☐ ☐

Yes   No

9. Labeling and mislabeling. You describe yourself, others, or an event with negative labels
such as "I'm a failure" or "He is a cheat."   ☐   ☐

10. Personalization. You identify and blame yourself as the cause of negative events or outcomes that you are not primarily responsible
for causing.   ☐   ☐

◇ **Cutting Down on Stress** ◇

1. Think of a time that you were feeling extremely stressed, and
write down all of your thoughts relating to this situation.

_____

_____

_____

2. Identify which, if any, of these thoughts match any of the
ten types of stressful thinking._____

_____

_____

_____

_____

3. Write down how you could rephrase your thinking so that
it is no longer stressful._____

_____

_____

_____

_____

◼ **BECOMING A MASTER SELF-LEADER** ◼

Are you ready to start improving your own performance
and happiness and that of your team? If you answered yes,
then some changes may be necessary. As someone wise
once stated, "If you always do what you've always done,
you always get what you've always got." So start practicing

self-leadership strategies in your life. Strive to become a master self-leader.

Becoming a master self-leader pulls together several of the self-leadership strategies we have presented. Here they are in summary form:

Summary of Self-Leadership Strategies

- **Preplay (mental imagery).** Practice important tasks in your mind before you do them.
- **Self-talk.** Examine and manage the way you talk to yourself to ensure it is constructive and helpful for your performance.
- **Managing your beliefs.** Examine and manage your beliefs to ensure they are accurate and constructive.
- **Self-observation.** Observe and gather information about specific behaviors that you have targeted for change.
- **Self–goal setting.** Set goals for your own work efforts.
- **Self-reward.** Provide yourself with personally valued rewards for completing desirable behaviors.
- **Build natural rewards into tasks and find the fun in your work.** Self-redesign of where and how you do your work will increase the level of natural rewards in your job. Natural rewards are part of rather than separate from the work (i.e., the work, like a hobby, becomes the reward).

Learning to put these strategies to work for you can be helpful for creating personal motivation and direction and achieving excellence. Before you become a true master self-leader, it is essential that you learn how to balance the variety of self-leadership strategies available. For example, becoming good at self–goal setting or self-reward can help you through difficult tasks that you don't naturally want to do. However, if you want to make your work more fun and motivating in its own right, strategies for building in natural rewards can help you create this situation. Managing your self-talk and beliefs or using preplay can be very helpful in achieving more constructive and positive thinking that will help you see through problems and recognize the opportunities they contain.

You can become a master self-leader by combining these different types of strategies to achieve a balance of self-discipline, natural enjoyment of your work, and constructive positive thinking. A practical four-step exercise will help you achieve a balanced, constructive application of the self-leadership strategies we have discussed. When you complete this exercise, you will have developed skills for effectively combining several strategies.[18]

◇ Learning Team Self-Leadership ◇

You can complete this exercise on your own, but it is especially effective when done with a team member or possibly in a group of three.

Select an area in which you would like to improve, one directly related to the job or to your personal life (if you improve aspects of your personal life, it is likely that the benefits you enjoy will carry over to your job as well, and vice versa). You may want to review some of your responses to other exercises you completed on team self-leadership strategies, particularly self–goal setting, or expand on an idea or issue you raised. Some examples of challenge areas are developing better relationships with coworkers, improving your physical fitness, improving your communication skills, going on a diet, quitting smoking, or developing more knowledge on a specific task.

The challenge area should address something that is important to you and that you sincerely want to improve on. Also, it should be something that you feel comfortable talking about with someone else (assuming that you are working with a partner).

Step 1

On the Self-Leadership Assessment Sheet (next page), write a description of your challenge with enough detail so that it is clear what you want to accomplish.

Then select some self-leadership strategies that make sense

Self-Leadership Assessment Sheet

Challenge Area: _____

Self-Leadership Strategies	How do you use?	How could you use?
Preplay (mental imagery)		
Self-talk		
Managing your beliefs		
Self-observation		
Self–goal setting		
Self-reward		
Build in natural rewards		

to you in addressing your challenge area. We recommend that you select about three strategies and that self–goal setting be one of them.

Step 2

If you are working with a partner, exchange assessment sheets. Take turns helping each other discover ways to apply the selected strategies to the challenge area. Focusing on one strategy at a time, ask your partner, "How do you use this strategy in other aspects of your life?" and "How could you use it to address your challenge area?" Take notes on what your partner says for later reference.

After discussing a strategy for you, then focus on a strategy for your team member. By working with a partner, you can ask questions and make suggestions to help each other develop a master self-leadership plan. Also, you can learn from each other by seeing how another person views self-leadership for making personal improvements.

After completing your conversation with your partner (typically lasting between forty-five and ninety minutes) return the other's Self-Leadership Assessment Sheet with notes you have written down for each other during your discussion.

Step 3

Review your notes on your Self-Leadership Assessment Sheet and what you learned while talking with your partner. Think about how you want to put each of your selected strategies to work in dealing with your challenge area and develop a plan.

Using the information from the Self-Leadership Assessment Sheet, work out a plan of self-leadership strategies that you can implement immediately. This plan will help you succeed in addressing your challenge area and ultimately to become a master self-leader.

Self-Leadership Plan

Challenge Area: _____

1. What is your goal? _____

_____

2. How soon do you want to achieve your goal?_____

_____

_____

3. What are your strategies?_____

_____

_____

_____

_____

_____

4. How can you use each strategy to address your challenge area?_____

_____

_____

_____

_____

5. How can you track your progress?_____

_____

_____

_____

_____

Step 4

Even the best-laid plans can fall apart; it's wise to anticipate the unexpected. Look at the two columns under "What If?" on page 88. In the first column, list anything you can think of that could interfere with successful implementation of your plan (e.g., temptations in your environment, peer pressure, other distractions, potential problems that could emerge). In the right column, write down the appropriate response to address the obstacles if they develop.

What if?

Potential Obstacles, Delays, and Slips	Plans to Overcome

Turn Your Weaknesses Into Strengths

Have you ever felt sorry for yourself
Because you thought you possessed a flaw?
Maybe you weren't as smart or attractive
As someone else you saw?

Then listen to this simple story.
I hope that you will do.
Because maybe it will change your mind
And alter your point of view.

There was a king whose source of power
Was a rare diamond, one of a kind.
But one day he dropped it; a scratch appeared;
The brilliant stone had lost its shine.

He tried and tried to make it right
But the scratch would not go away.
An old man volunteered to give it a shot.
He would come back the very next day.

When the old man returned to the castle,
The king beamed like a radiant sun.
The diamond was now more stunning than ever;
And this is what the old man had done.

A beautiful rose was so elegantly carved
On the face of the gem.
And the ugly scratch that was once a flaw,
Now served as the stem.

The moral of this quaint little tale
Is that by altering your frame of mind,
Your imperfections will no longer exist.
Success you soon will find.

(continues)

(*continued*)

Your faults can be your best assets
If you perceive them this way.
They can actually be the catalyst
Toward achievement everyday.

So don't dwell on what you don't have
Or ponder the "scratches" on you.
By turning your weaknesses into strengths,
Your dreams will one day come true.
—Christopher P. Neck

4

TEAM TALK

A variety of effective communication
techniques that allow for an open productive and conflict-managed arena for
the exchange of ideas within the team

Learning About Team Talk
Speak Up!
Helping Others to Speak Up
Do You Hear What I Hear?
Treating Other Team Members the Way
    They Want to Be Treated
Building Bridges of Trust

◢ LEARNING ABOUT TEAM TALK ◢

Communication is the bridge over which team members share ideas, influence action, and build healthy working relationships. When communication is effective, team members connect with each other and collaborate in achieving the team's mission. When communication is ineffective, bridges turn into barriers, teams do not function effectively, and frustration results. In short, it is imperative that team members talk and that the team talk is effective in achieving the outcomes of the team and its members.

Read the list that follows and place a checkmark in the column that best describes you.

◇ ◇ ◇

	Yes	No	At Times
I am aware of my communication style and its effect on others.	☐	☐	☐
I can comfortably say what needs to be said without causing hostility.	☐	☐	☐
I have the ability to encourage others to speak up with comfort.	☐	☐	☐
I listen effectively and retain ideas quite well.	☐	☐	☐
I am conscious of treating others the way they want to be treated.	☐	☐	☐
I can make choices that inspire others to trust me.	☐	☐	☐
I can provide team leadership in problem solving.	☐	☐	☐

If several of your marks were "no" or "at times," then prepare to find some concrete suggestions that will move you closer to being a better team communicator.

What's Your Communication Style?

"How do I get others to do their share of the work?" "How do I make them willing to participate?" "How do I influence these guys to buy in?" These questions are like many others we have heard while listening to employees just like you who seem worried about going it alone in a self-managed environment.

In a self-managed work team, there are no bosses around to make sure that your team members do their job as it ought to be done, so it's up to you to talk to your team members in a manner that will get a commitment from them. Think about the last time you were in the presence of coworkers who were not performing effectively. Were you passive and so uncomfortable that you didn't say anything? Were you aggressive or pushy, telling others how things ought to be whether they liked it or not? Were you assertive in saying what needed to be said without generating hostility? Whether you were passive, aggressive, or assertive, you demonstrated a communication style, and the style you used probably made a difference in the success of your communication and the impact on your team members. We recommend an assertive conversational style as a means of talking to team members in a manner that will yield the best results.

When team members are assertive, they stand up for themselves and speak their mind without becoming uncomfortable and without putting other people down. Assertive people usually let you know where they stand. We believe that an assertive communication style is typically the most effective approach to team talk in that it is more likely to result in a win-win situation.

In contrast, passive people have some trouble speaking up on their own behalf or making requests of others. You may know some people in your shop, at the next machine, or at the next desk who tend to be passive. They do their own work quite well, but it is just not comfortable for them to tell other members of the team what to do—or make suggestions to anyone else for that matter. If these passive people cannot find a way to speak up, they can defeat the purpose of an empowered work climate. Their interactions are often lose-win, and the team loses the benefit of their insights. Self-management works best when people are willing to take advantage of the influence they are given. In a team environment, everyone must pull his or her share of the load, and that applies to speaking up just as much as it applies to doing the assigned tasks.

Just as a team will likely have at least one person who cannot speak up and say what needs to be said, most teams also seem to have an aggressive person who gives you his opinion whether you want it or not. Like assertive people, aggressive people stand up for themselves without being shy or embarrassed, but they rarely worry about the impact they have on others. They often say and do what they wish regardless of who is hurt by it. They can be just as destructive to a self-directed environment as can passive people. On the manufacturing floor or in the office, aggressive people are hard to live with. The tendency is to get out of their way even if it means bidding out to another job. The problem is that high mobility does not build the trust essential to teams or contribute to a sense of community within the workplace.

◇ Discovering Your Communication Style ◇

To see whether your communication style fits into the pattern of passive, assertive, or aggressive behavior, examine the following activities as they would apply to your working community. In front of each statement mark **P** for passive, **A** for assertive, or **AG** for aggressive as a way of indicating the communication style you would typically use in each situation. Respond not as you think you *should* respond but as you actually behave in such situations.

_____ A coworker borrowed some of your tools a week ago and has not returned them.

_____ A team member has not cleaned his machine for so long that there is a risk of breakdown.

_____ A team member leaves the workplace early every day.

_____ You are not getting clear direction from upper management.

_____ A fellow worker keeps blaming others for your group's being behind schedule.

_____ Team members are being stretched to the limit; they are overworked and undermotivated.

_____ The specialist in your area is not in the shop often enough.

_____ There is a know-it-all on your team who stifles most discussions during team meetings.

_____ A team member does excellent work in your area but never cleans up after herself.

_____ A team member has never read the literature on self-directed work teams, and her ignorance shows in her behavior; she doesn't have a clue as to what it's about.

Interpretation

If most of your answers were **A** (assertive), you probably are making an excellent contribution to your team in saying what needs to be said without generating hostility. If you marked several as **P** (passive) or **AG** (aggressive), you may want to consider using assertiveness for your own satisfaction and the sake of your team. Keep reading. We'll be looking at how to use more desirable communication throughout this Team Talk section.

◤ SPEAK UP! ◤

There are five steps to assertive problem solving that you can use in saying what needs to be said in almost any situation:

1. Communicating caring or empathy for the other person's situation.

2. Describing the particular problem area without being evaluative or judgmental.
3. Describing the effects of the problem area on the team, the task, or the mission.
4. Requesting a specific change in behavior.
5. Being willing to compromise.[19]

Keep in mind that steps for assertive problem solving are based on the assumption that most people listen and respond more effectively if they feel valued.

Step 1: Communicating Caring or Empathy for the Other Person's Situation

If another team member is not cleaning his equipment or maintains a messy or even hazardous work area, a passive team member would probably look the other way. In contrast, an aggressive team member would have no patience for communicating caring or empathy and would probably go straight to the bottom line in an almost pushy way. In fact, aggressive members of seminars we have put on have often accused us of soft-soaping the other person when we suggest that caring or empathy should be the first step in this problem-solving approach. If soft-soaping is designed to reduce friction, then perhaps it's an appropriate term, because we do believe that people listen more effectively and respond more cooperatively when they feel valued than when they are defensive.

Communicating that you care about the other person may be as simple as reminding the person of the amount of time you've worked together and how much you've appreciated the camaraderie during this time or how much you value the quality of work that the other person has always produced. Empathy can be described as "feeling with" the other person. It is often communicated by stating what you believe the other person is feeling at the moment. The feeling could be frustration, disappointment, stress, or enthusiasm. In either case, as you approach the individual to discuss the problem, your first words should be designed to reinforce the relationship before you talk about the content that is of concern.

Step 2: Describing the Behavior Without Being Evaluative or Judgmental

A descriptive statement tells your team member what you've observed. It doesn't indicate that what you've observed is good or bad, right or wrong. A descriptive statement differs from an evaluative statement in that it doesn't impose your value system on the other person's behavior. It is simply a reflection of what you have noticed. When using a descriptive statement to describe the climate in your workplace, you might say "It's about 68 degrees in here," whereas when using an evaluative statement, you might say, "They made this area too cold." Most of us will listen objectively to a team member's description of a situation but tend to defend against a comment we see as a personal criticism of our actions. For example, the person who controls the thermostat is likely to be less defensive on hearing the first comment than the second.

In using an evaluative statement, I might simply tell Chuck, "Your work area is messy." A descriptive statement, in contrast, would be a statement of what I observed, not my judgment as to whether it is good or bad—for example, "I've noticed that a lot of scrap pieces have spilled over into the aisle." "I" language is an important part of description. It allows the team member to listen to what "I observed" rather that what "he or she did" and therefore has less potential for creating a defensive response. If you hear yourself starting to talk about a behavior with "you didn't" or "you shouldn't," chances are you are heading toward a statement that may be viewed as a judgment rather than a description, and it may cause trouble.

Step 3: Describing the Effects of the Problem Area

You want to make a team member aware of the implications of what he has been doing. In this step, you should phrase your comments so the team member hears an objective description of the effects that have been observed or experienced and not an effort to take pot shots at his performance. For example, you might say, "I find myself feeling frustrated," or "I have trouble getting down the aisle," not, "You make me frustrated" or "You're making a mess all over the aisle." An important part of assertiveness is to realize that you must own your feelings. In other words, the other person behaves and you are entitled to react to the behavior, but no one really "makes" you feel or do anything.

There is an assumption here that if you have a fairly good relationship with a team member and something he is doing is resulting in discomfort for others, then he will want to correct the situation in order to reduce that discomfort. These steps work best if the person you are trying to influence has some stake in the matter and would prefer that your working life be more comfortable rather than miserable. If this is the case, upon hearing the effects of the condition you've described, the offending team member should be ready to hear the next step.

Step 4: Requesting a Specific Change in Behavior

Before introducing this issue with the team member, know exactly what you would like to be changed. Now that you have prepared your listener and she is receptive to your ideas, this is the time to exert your influence on her behavior. Request a specific change in behavior by letting her know exactly what you would like to have happen. Since assertive individuals are determined to express themselves without denying the rights of others, this step must be phrased as a request and not a demand, command, or threat. There should not be a tone of, "You'd better start doing this, or else" but rather a tone of mutual respect and appreciation. The request for a change in behavior might be phrased as, "I'd really appreciate it if the scrap from the machine could be stacked in the corner until it's picked up by maintenance. Would that be comfortable for you?"

If you demand a change from a peer team member, you might be met with resistance, hostility, and defensiveness. But when you *request* a change, the phrasing is such that the team member feels free to say no. In such cases, you need to be open to compromise.

Step 5: Being Willing to Compromise

Teams function most effectively in an atmosphere of mutual respect. Letting your team member know that you are willing to compromise is a way to communicate that respect. The compromise does not have to be a sophisticated process; it can be a simple matter of give and take. When a team member cannot comply with your request, perhaps the best approach is to return to the statement of the effects: "I understand you are overworked, but no one can get down the aisle and it could be a fire hazard. How do you think we should handle this?"

Most team members have solutions they are willing to share in solving a problem. In a high percentage of the cases we've experienced, as soon as you make your request known, the team member will probably say, "No problem." If the person cannot comply with your request for change, he may have an alternative suggestion that solves the problem just as well. The compromise enables both you and your team member to move toward a win-win result. Try putting some of these steps into practice with this exercise.

◇ Learning How to Speak Up ◇

Think of a situation in your work community where you believe that life would be a lot better if a team member would change his or her behavior. Work through the steps we suggest, visualizing yourself actually talking to the person, but make sure you are clear, concise, and to the point. Write one sentence for each step to show what you would say.

The Situation: _____

_____

_____

1. Communicate caring for the person or empathy for his or
   her situation (e.g., "Anne, we've been working together for
   quite a few years now, and I've always admired the pride
   which you take in your work," or, "I know how frustrating
   it must be to have all of this work piling up, especially since
   no one but you has been certified on this machine").

   _____

   _____

   _____

   _____

2. Describe the problem behavior without being evaluative or
   judgmental (e.g., "I've noticed that a lot of scrap pieces
   have spilled over into the aisle").

   _____

   _____

   _____

   _____

3. Describe the effects of this condition in terms of feelings
   or practical problems (e.g., "I find myself feeling frustrated
   because I have trouble getting down the aisle").

   _____

   _____

   _____

   _____

4. Request a specific and concrete change in behavior (e.g.,
   "I'd really appreciate it if the scrap from the machine could

be stacked in the corner until it is picked up by maintenance. Would that be okay with you?").

_____

_____

_____

_____

5. Be willing to compromise by requesting an alternative solution from the other person if your solution is not comfortable for him or her (e.g., "If my idea won't work for you
then how do you think we should handle this?").

_____

_____

_____

_____

In completing the exercise, you expressed an assertive
communication style that enabled you to say what needs
to be said to others with a minimal risk of generating defensiveness. It's important to practice these steps before
actually expressing them to the individual. It is also important that you speak to the person privately and allow
your voice, face, and body to be as assertive as your words.
Maintain direct eye contact, an erect posture, and a facial
expression that matches your ideas.

◪ HELPING OTHERS TO SPEAK UP ◪

You can help to create a team environment where others
feel comfortable speaking up by using one or more of the
following communication skills in team meetings and one-
to-one interactions with team members: openness, empathy, positiveness, supportiveness, and equality.[20] We've dis-

covered that using one or more of these skills adds a sense of safety and comfort to any relationship resulting in team members' feeling secure enough to speak up—a quality that is essential to effective teams.

Openness

Openness involves being willing to share ideas and feelings with other team members. For some people, openness is natural, but for others it is not. Nevertheless, it is easier for others to be open if you take the risk of being open with them. When we are open, it often inspires openness in others, promotes closeness, and even reduces tension. Think of a time when you had something on your mind that was bothering you. Wasn't there a sense of relief when someone else mentioned the same issue? Whether we call it clearing the air, leveling, or laying our cards on the table, openness gives a sense of relief and is often a contagious behavior. Team members will "catch it" and be more likely to speak up.

◇ Opening Up ◇

Take a break with a team member, and go to an area where you are not likely to be interrupted. Take turns with your partner in completing these statements. Turn taking is essential to establishing trust, so neither of you should give long speeches.

1. My name is . . .

2. In my family there are . . .

3. My favorite pastime is . . .

4. When I'm in a new group I . . .

5. The first day on a new job I usually feel . . .

6. I am happiest at work when I . . .

7. What turns me off the most about work is . . .

8. When I'm criticized I usually . . .

9. I worry most about . . .

10. Generally right now I feel . . .

We have found that whenever any of us does this exercise with another person, there is a little discomfort in the beginning, but it subsides as we both realize that there are more similarities than differences in what we are thinking and feeling. The idea that we are alone in our thoughts and feelings can prevent us from sharing ideas, but having the confidence of knowing that others might be experiencing the same thing is an important step toward helping us to speak up.

Empathy

Our second skill, *empathy,* is the best skill for connecting with another team member. It ensures understanding, prevents confusion, and encourages others to feel confident in speaking up. In our experience, the confidence that empathy brings to others stems from their belief that another person cares enough to make an effort to relate; hence the person reasons, "I can take the risk of sharing a little more about myself because it seems as though the empathic person won't mind listening."

The difficulty in expressing empathy seems to lie in the skill level. We have heard many people use the phrases, "I know how you feel," "I've been there," "Tell me about it," or "Welcome to the club," as efforts at connecting with another person. Some of these phrases may be well intentioned, but they seldom give the receiver a green light that says, "I really heard what you are feeling, and I am here if you want to speak up a little more."

We have found that the best way to let a team member know that you sense what he or she is feeling is to express a word that you think captures that feeling. To do this, re-member that most of us share more similarities than differ-ences; then think of a time when you might have been going through something similar to what your team mem-ber is experiencing and recall how you felt at the moment. Was it frustration, excitement, disappointment, worry, con-cern, anger, or relief? Once you've identified the feeling, express it as your understanding of what the other person may be going through.

◇ **Practicing Empathic Responses** ◇

Look at each statement and recall a time when you may have gone through a similar experience. Remember what you were feeling at that time. Then, express that feeling in words that are directed at the team member and phrase those words as a suggestion of what the team member must be going through rather than focusing on yourself. We'll do the first two as sam-ples, and you do the rest.

Statement: "How do I get others to do their share of the work?"

Empathic response: "You seem frustrated that everyone is not pitching in."

Statement: "How do I make them willing to participate?"

Empathic response: "Their reluctance to teaming seems pretty uncomfortable for you."

Statement: "Managers and workers need to be able to speak honestly about what ticks them off."

Empathic response: _____

_____

Statement: "We need open, honest communication."

Empathic response: _____

_____

Statement: "It's a challenge to be peer to peer with a person who was previously your boss."
Empathic response: _____
_____

You may feel as though you are stating the obvious when you empathize by paraphrasing what you believe the other person is feeling. However, the value comes from the fact that your team member knows that someone else is trying to connect and someone else cares. If your empathic response sends this message, then you are well on your way to helping another team member speak up a little more. The mutual sharing of ideas and feelings that empathy generates promotes the synergy and bonding essential to effective teaming.

Positiveness

Positiveness can be an important skill in creating a comfortable team climate and helping other team members speak up. When you use positiveness, you are looking at what is right about a situation or person rather than focusing on what is wrong about it. Positiveness does not mean being unrealistic, putting your head in the sand, or filling the air with clichés such as, "It's always darkest before the dawn." What we do mean is realistically evaluating the condition and finding an aspect or two that you have going for you.

Think about the last time you felt a little down in the dumps or depressed. Wasn't it of value to have someone close by who had a slightly different perspective on things? In our personal lives, we often expose our children, other family members, and friends to our positive view of their circumstance. Team members sometimes need the same kind of feedback. When they listen to your positive point of view, it not only gives them a new outlook, but it inspires confidence in the team environment and a willingness to open up about other issues.

Positiveness can be contagious. If you are positive with team members, they too will be more inclined to speak up in positive ways. When you are positive, you send a message that things are okay, and when things are okay, everyone finds it a little easier to open up. Positiveness not only gives everyone the confidence to be open, but it also draws everyone closer to the source of the positiveness. A team member who expresses positive messages is often a magnet to which others are drawn, a hero who brings the hero out of other team members as well.

◇ Practicing Positive Responses ◇

Write a positive response to each negative comment. We will do the first one, you complete the balance.

Negative comment: "No way in hell will this ever work."

Positive response: "Maybe we're just in a storming phase. Two teams are working well."

Negative comment: "We can't get realistic reviews from peers."

Positive response: _____

_____

Negative comment: "If we're self-directed, why are the managers still here?"

Positive response: _____

_____

Negative comment: "You can't empower people if you don't have the power to give them."

Positive response: _____

_____

Your responses to these comments would be viewed by most as being positive if you focused on what was right about the situation or the person rather than focusing on what was wrong. If team members are able to be positive more often, other team members will catch the positive confidence and feel more comfortable speaking up.

There may be times when it is difficult to think of a positive response to a negative comment. At times like this, you need not sit back silently at a loss for words. In fact, it may encourage other team members to speak up if you communicate in a supportive way.

Supportiveness

A *supportive* statement is one that validates a person's right to honest feelings or thoughts. It is not a statement of agreement about the message the team member is communicating but rather a reinforcement of the team member's right to state the message.

Think of a time when you may have held an unpopular position. Did you wish that someone would call a time-out and validate your right to hold that position? Read the following sentence aloud stating your name. "I'm not sure I agree with what [*your first name*] is saying, but I think its only fair that we hear her out." Would you feel a little closer to the person who validated you with this statement? Would you be more inclined to want to speak up and say your piece? If so, you have just experienced a major effect of a supportive comment.

Because validating a person's right tends to boost the person's self-image, a supportive response is often viewed as one that reduces tension and defuses defensiveness. When tension is reduced and defensiveness is defused, most of us feel more comfortable speaking up. We encourage you to incorporate supportiveness within your repertoire of responses and communicate it to other team members at appropriate times. We are fairly certain that you will be seen as a constructive force in enabling team members to be more open in sharing the ideas, which the entire team needs if it is to accomplish its mission.

Equality

Self-managed teams often create a leveling factor within an organization. When senior employees and former bosses move to self-direction, they may find that they are working in a peer relationship with team members who have just been hired into the organization. In such an environment, there is a strong tendency for the more experienced people to remind others of their years in the business and their many achievements. This type of communication can be intimidating to employees who do not share this status within the company. Such intimidation can lead new team members to close down and not communicate.

In order to help new team members speak up, it is often essential for more experienced team members to forget the differences between themselves and the new team members and focus on the similarities. This communication skill is referred to as *equality.*

Equality involves communicating to others as though everyone is on the same level. It is characterized by "we" messages and statements of common ground. Most of us have a sense of discomfort when we encounter someone who comes across as being superior. "Superior" people create discomfort because they seem compelled to remind us of how much better they are than the rest of us in terms of age, money, status, education, or intellect. If you know of inequalities between you and other team members, we advise you to keep them to yourself and emphasize similarities. It will create a nonthreatening climate and boost the self-worth of new team members, prompting them to speak up.

It is important that openness, empathy, positiveness, supportiveness, and equality be in your repertoire of ways to respond to other team members. It you take advantage of opportunities to use these skills, you can help to create a team environment where others feel comfortable sharing ideas. This is the foundation for the synergy that every team must have for its success.

The following exercise is designed to help you practice the interpersonal skills that will assist others in speaking up.

◇ Honing Your Interpersonal Skills ◇

A fellow team member says to you, "I don't feel as though I'm getting much accomplished at work anymore." Respond in five ways, each expressing a different skill.

1. Your response demonstrating *openness* (sharing your own ideas and feelings).

_____

_____

_____

2. Your response demonstrating *empathy* (verbalizing what you believe the other person to be feeling).

_____

_____

_____

3. Your response demonstrating *positiveness* (focusing on what is right about the situation or person).

_____

_____

_____

4. Your response demonstrating *supportiveness* (validating the other person's right to feel or think in that way).

_____

_____

_____

5. Your response demonstrating *equality* (establishing a common ground by stressing similarities and emphasizing that you are on a plateau similar to that of the team member).

_____

_____

_____

◪ DO YOU HEAR WHAT I HEAR? ◪

Before you continue reading, answer the following questions, numbered from 1 to 10. Because speed is important, work as quickly as possible. Do exactly what each question asks you to do. Now start and do questions 1 and 10. When you are finished, put your pencil down and continue reading this book.

1. Write your name. _____

2. Add 63789 and 98765. _____

3. Subtract 94872 from 95467. _____

4. Stand up and sit down.

5. Clap your hands three times.

6. Say, "It's a great day," out loud four times.

7. Write the last seven letters of the alphabet. _____

8. Say these words to yourself, "I'm almost finished! I've followed directions."

9. Multiply 896 by 698. _____

10. Write your phone number backward. _____

You are probably wondering why we asked you to perform this exercise. Before we answer this question, we'd like to ask you one: Did you perform all ten steps of this exercise? If you didn't, congratulations for listening carefully. If you did, go back to the instructions, and reread them slowly and thoroughly. Gotcha! If you really listened to our instructions you would have performed only items 1 *and* 10 of the exercise, not items 1 *through* 10.

Our aim was not to trick you but to illustrate an important point: Many times in our daily lives, we don't listen as well as we should. We may hear what a fellow team member is saying to us, but too often we don't listen. Hearing is a passive activity; listening requires you to be active, figuring out what someone is trying to convey to you. In the exercise you just did, you may have performed poorly and completed all ten items because you were not listening fully. In the same way, if you and your team members are poor listeners, conflict or poor performance may be a problem—if not now, probably in time. In fact, communication experts argue that listening skills are important to success on the job and in your personal life.

Ask yourself whether during the past week you have pretended to listen to a team member's conversation when actually you were only pretending to listen by nodding your head at regular intervals or saying, "Yeah" or "Uh huh?" If you answered yes, you have plenty of company. The truth is that many times we pretend to listen and miss important information.

You can learn listening skills. You and your team members can improve your listening habits in order to improve your individual success and your team's success.

The following specific suggestions can help you and your team members be more effective listeners:

1. Clear your mind and relax. This can help you focus on what someone else is saying rather than on something else in your mind.

2. Make eye contact. By making eye contact, you let the other person know that you are interested in what she is saying. Eye contact can help you focus on what the speaker is saying rather than on distracting thoughts.

3. Avoid focusing solely on first words. Most listening mistakes are made when you hear only the first few words of someone's sentence. You finish the sentence in your own mind, and miss the second portion of the speaker's sentence.

4. Always paraphrase. Restate in your own words to the speaker what she is saying, feeling, or meaning. Use phrases like, "What I hear you saying is . . ." or "In other words, you mean . . ." By doing this, you are able to check yourself in terms you were listening or just hearing the speaker's words.

5. Don't cut the speaker off. If you cut the speaker off before he is able to complete his thoughts, you signal that you were guessing where the speaker's thoughts were going and that you were not completely listening.

6. Avoid talking too much. We all like to talk about ourselves, but if we talk too much, we don't have time to listen. One way to be a better listener is to avoid talking too much. It is impossible to talk and listen at the same time.

7. Pay attention to nonverbal communication. A lot of what someone is trying to say to you comes not from the voice but from nonverbal sources such as facial expressions, voice tone, or posture. Pay attention to all signals.

8. Remind yourself by using positive self-talk. The moment you start feeling distracted when you are trying to listen, tell yourself, "This is important. Keep your eye contact on the speaker. Don't mess with pens or pencils. Stay focused."

9. Practice. Practice these tips over and over as you attempt to listen rather than hear what someone is trying to tell you. Using these new listening skills within your team will help you all become successful listeners and work together more effectively.

◪ TREAT OTHER TEAM MEMBERS THE WAY ◪ *THEY* WANT TO BE TREATED

The way in which you talk to other team members can make the difference between success or failure in your day-to-day team interactions. Treating team members with respect protects their self-worth and can inspire their cooperation. If you don't select your team talk carefully, your words can chip away at your coworkers' self-esteem, and they will build a wall of defensiveness to protect themselves. When defensiveness occurs, it usually means trouble for the team. There is little incentive to cooperate with a team member whom we believe to be attacking us. Let's see how effective you are at selecting words that protect others' self-esteem.[21]

◇ Selecting Words to Protect Others' ◇ Self-Esteem

For each set of statements, circle the **P** if you believe the statement communicates the message in a manner that *protects* the self-esteem of the team member receiving the message and the **D** if the statement has more of a potential to *diminish* the team member's self-worth.

Set 1

P   D   "That report doesn't concern me, so I couldn't care less how it's set up. Just do what you want to do."

P   D   "You must feel good to know that you have written the data in such a way as to make your report easy for the reader to follow and remember."

Set 2

P   D   "Those ideas for the project are pretty good, Jim, but Beth and I worked through the project the other day, and we've already selected the ideas we want to use."

P   D   "Jim, Beth and I started to come up with some ideas for the project, but we held off because we thought it best if all ideas are shared at once. What are your thoughts?"

Set 3
P   D   "Up to this point, it seems as though you've based your decision on all of the data available."

P   D   "Your decision is limited by your data, which are also limited."

Set 4
P   D   "I've already made some decisions, but if she has some new input, it's worth taking some time to consider it. I may have been wrong."

P   D   "I've made up my mind. I'm not about to accept any suggestions she has to offer at this late date."

Set 5
P   D   "You'd better read the specifications and then come back to the next team meeting with a better understanding than you have now."

P   D   "We could probably all use a better understanding of this problem than we have now. If we reexamine those specifications, it might help us solve the problem."

Set 6
P   D   "A few of us have worked here a lot longer than you people have. If you think you can come up with a better idea, you've got a lot to learn."

P   D   "We all come from differing frames of reference and experiences. The background of our older team members along with the fresh perspectives of our newer members should give us a broad base from which to draw new ideas."

Interpretation

Now compare your responses with the choices we have identified. Out of context, it is difficult to label the statements accurately as those that would protect the self-image or dimish it, so note the analysis we used in making our choices.

Set 1

P Ⓓ "That report doesn't concern me, so I couldn't care less how it's set up. Just do what you want to do."

Ⓟ D "It must be a good feeling to know that you have written the data in such a way as to make your report easy for the reader to follow and remember."

We've identified the first statement as potentially diminishing to the self-esteem because the words "doesn't concern me," "couldn't care less," and "do what you want to do," are usually perceived as indifferent. They suggest that the other team member isn't sufficiently valuable to waste our time on her.

The second statement is more likely to protect the receiver's self-image because the team member who is making the statement is taking enough time to empathize with her coworker. The empathy is communicated in the phrase, "It must be a good feeling to know . . ." Empathy can be a boon to the person's self-esteem because it tells the receiver that she is important enough for someone to want to take the time to connect with her feelings.

Set 2

P Ⓓ "Those ideas for the project are pretty good, Jim, but Beth and I worked through the project the other day, and we've already selected the ideas we want to use."

Ⓟ D "Jim, Beth and I started to come up with some ideas for the project, but we held off because we thought it best if all ideas are shared at once. What are your thoughts?"

The first statement may be perceived as diminishing because the team member could believe that his ideas didn't matter. If his ideas did matter, then perhaps his team members would have waited until he expressed his views before making a decision. There is a degree of defensiveness that the receiver of this message could experience because he wasted both time and energy by creating and presenting an idea after the decisions were already made.

Since we wait for important people to be present before making decisions, we saw the second sentence as one that would protect the team member's self-esteem. The message suggests that the receiver and his ideas are valued because the problem-solving process that was used ensured that the key players were present before decisions were made. Part of treating people the way they want to be treated is letting them know they are so valued that we will wait for them before making important decisions.

Set 3

Ⓟ   D   "Up to this point it seems as though you've based your decision on all of the data available.

P   Ⓓ   "Your decision is limited by your data, which are also limited."

If you've identified the first sentence as one that would protect the team member's self-image, you may have done so because the statement is a pure description of the sender's perception. Descriptive statements usually protect the recipient's self-image because they avoid any suggestion that what the other person did was right or wrong, good or bad. Descriptive statements are observations, not criticisms. They provide nothing to defend against.

In contrast, the second sentence, which we've identified as potentially diminishing to the self-image, is an implied judgment about the decision that was made and the data gathering that was done. It is likely that when a team member believes that he is being criticized, it can be a blow to the self-esteem. He may fight back or defend himself to protect his self-worth. The defense may be as mild as the silent treatment, which communicates, "If I don't talk, you can't criticize me," or as aggressive as a countercriticism or a counterattack.

Treating team members the way they want to be treated means avoiding overtly critical or evaluative statements and substituting descriptive statements. It is just as easy to say, "Our goal for this month is sixty units, and we've completed forty," as it is to say, "You're way behind schedule." Most people would rather be treated with the objectivity of the first statement than the criticism of the second.

Set 4

Ⓟ D   "I've already made some decisions, but if she has some new input, it's worth taking some time to consider it. I may have been wrong."

P Ⓓ   "I've made up my mind. I'm not about to accept any suggestions she has to offer at this late date."

The first sentence is thought to protect the self-image because it tells the team member that the person who sent the message is open to her ideas and allows the team member to feel valuable. Note the use of the phrase, "I may have been wrong." This is referred to as a *provisional statement*. It qualifies the information being communicated as being based on the sender's perception. Provisional qualifiers include adding one of the following phrases to your informative message: "In my opinion," "Based on my experience," "According to the research I've examined," "I may be wrong," or "It seems to me." These phrases suggest to the team member who hears them that the person delivering the message is acknowledging that someone else may have a different point of view. That acknowledgment is an indicator of the respect that most members would like to receive.

The second sentence is more the statement of a know-it-all, a person who is closed to anyone else's point of view. Team members like to be treated as though they have something to add to the team. Know-it-all comments deny them that value. It is sometimes difficult for knowledgeable people to avoid coming across in a dogmatic, know-it-all manner. The key is the ability to state knowledge in provisional ways.

Set 5

P Ⓓ   "You'd better read the specifications and then come
              back to the next team meeting with a better under-
              standing than you have now."

Ⓟ D   "We could probably all use a better understanding of
              this problem than we have now. If we re-
              examine those specifications, it might help us solve
              the problem."

We identified the first statement as one that would be likely
to diminish a team member's self-esteem because of the controlling language within the message. In stating, "You'd better
read . . . and then come back," one team member is verbally
pushing the other around. A team member confronted by such
language usually responds in a defensive way, reasoning "Since
most important people are not pushed around, I had better
push back or defend to protect the self-image that I have left."
Controlling language is the language of the traditional Strongman style of leadership. It is *not* the way most team members
wish to be treated.

If you find that it is difficult to speak in a manner that is
not as controlling, practice talking to your team members
about the conditions that you all face rather than telling them
what ought to be done about the conditions. This approach,
often referred to as being problem oriented instead of control
oriented, is based on the assumption that intelligent, informed
people who are faced with a problem usually evolve a solution
without being told how it ought to be done. Notice that in the
second sentence in Set 5, the speaker is making an effort to
protect the self-image of the person being spoken to by saying,
"We could probably all use a better understanding of the problem," rather than insisting that the other team members "read
the specifications."

Remember that your fellow team members regularly make
important decisions within their families and their social
groups. Sharing a problem with them rather than dictating the
answer comes closer to treating them in the way in which they
want to be treated.

Set 6

P Ⓓ   "A few of us have worked here a lot longer than you

people have. If you think you can come up with a better idea, you've got a lot to learn."

(P) D   "We all come from differing frames of reference and experiences. The background of our older team members along with the fresh perspectives of our newer members should give us a broad base from which to draw new ideas."

The first sentence in Set 6 is identified as the one more likely to diminish self-esteem because it places the team member who hears it on a slightly lower status than the speaker. On a human worth scale, we like to think of ourselves as being equal in value and merit to those around us. When a fellow team member reminds us of the differences in age, experience, education, or compensation, it can be seen as a put-down, and we will fight back or defend the self-esteem that is being threatened.

Notice that the second sentence protects the self-image of the receiving team member by emphasizing the value the less experienced team members bring to the table. The comment places all team members on the same plateau and suggests that there is strength in diversity. It is easier to listen to people who value our differences than to those who criticize those differences.

A most important part of treating other team members the way they want to be treated is respect. Every time you interact with other team members, you can communicate that respect by making language choices that protect their self-esteem. When you communicate in these ways, you are more likely to inspire the kind of commitment that will make the team stronger than the sum of its parts as the members move cooperatively toward their objectives.

◢ BUILDING BRIDGES OF TRUST ◢

Recently one of us had to find a body shop for the family car—and quickly. It was also important to select a trust-

worthy body shop, so we checked out two body shops rec-
ommended by a friend, visiting each briefly. The decision
was easy. Body Shop B inspired trust; Body Shop A did
not. As you read, see if you can identify the aspects that
influenced trust or its lack.

We made two telephone calls to Body Shop A. Each
time we were placed on hold for an indefinite period, so
we decided that a visit to Body Shop A might be faster.
When we got to the office, no one was there to greet us at
the counter. Several employees dressed in attire indicating
they worked at the body shop walked by us without acknowledging our presence. Finally, after shouting "hello"
several times, an employee sauntered out from a back
room. When we inquired about the work we needed, his
responses were indefinite. Moreover, he seemed to be shuffling papers on the countertop rather than making eye contact with us, his potential customers. We took a business
card, said we might call back later, and walked out the
door, never to return.

When we called Body Shop B, a clerk answered after
the second ring and immediately connected us with the
manager. He seemed after a brief description to know exactly the kind of damage that had been done to the car and
told us that if we would come down to the shop, he would
be waiting for us. Within minutes, we were in the car driv-
ing to Body Shop B. When we arrived, we introduced ourselves to the first person we saw. He was the manager with
whom we had spoken. He shook hands firmly, then listened, while looking us directly in the eyes, to a brief description of our circumstance. He picked up a pad and
said, "Let's see what we can do to help you out." As we
followed him out the door to the car, he began asking questions and taking notes. We left with a concrete image of
what needed to be done and specific directions as to what
to tell our insurance company. We received a follow-up call
from Body Shop B on the following morning.

Body Shop B was the vendor of choice. The shop was
successful in capturing our business because the employ-

ees inspired trust. Take a few minutes to reread our story. Then list five characteristics communicated by Body Shop B that you believe were influential in inspiring trust:

1. _____

2. _____

3. _____

4. _____

4. _____

5. _____

See if the characteristics you wrote down are similar to those we believe inspired our trust.

1. Attentiveness. Body Shop A seemed unattentive in several ways: The employees never answered the telephone; when we walked into the shop, a number of employees walked right by us without acknowledging our presence; and when an employee did surface, he never made eye contact. In American culture, a lack of eye contact can be a sign of inattentiveness and is also associated with not listening.

In contrast, the employees of Body Shop B communicated attentiveness by picking up the telephone by the second ring; the manager offered a firm handshake during the first personal encounter, maintaining direct eye contact as we began to describe the damage, and doing some notetaking, which suggested listening. The attentiveness of Body Shop B was a definite factor in establishing trust. We tend to trust people who seem to care about us.

2. Energy. The several employees who walked through the area at Body Shop A did so in a manner suggesting they would rather be somewhere else. That may have been what they were feeling, but communicating that attitude also communicates that a lazy work ethic might be applied in the shop as employees work on vehicles. Even the employee who responded to our call for help sauntered out to the customer contact area in a way that suggested little, if any, physical energy. It is hard to trust people who seem to lack passion for what they are doing.

What a difference we discovered at Body Shop B. The clerk answered the telephone with positive energy in her voice, and the manager moved about the area as though he were on a mission. Their vocal and physical energy suggested that they knew what they were doing and were eager to do it.

3. Openness. It is difficult to trust people whom you don't know, and the employees at Body Shop A shared virtually no information. The employees who walked by us did not even offer a hello. The mutual sharing of information requires some degree of risk in that people may use the information against us or use it to manipulate us, but it also communicates trust. As a comparison, when we lend someone an object of value, there is the risk that it may not be returned or may be damaged. When the item is returned safely, our trust of the other person usually increases. Information follows the same pattern as objects. Information openly exchanged provides the potential for trust to develop.

With no openness at Body Shop A, there was no potential for trust to develop. The manager at Body Shop B was open about his years of service with the company, his experience with our insurance company, and his understanding of the frustration we were experiencing. The mutual sharing of information led to a sense of mutual trust.

4. Knowledge. Having knowledge and expertise about the subject being discussed inspires trust. Whether the person is a doctor, professor, mechanic, or food server, it is hard to trust someone who doesn't seem to know what he is talking about. Clearly our contact at Body Shop A, who spent his time shuffling through papers, gave us no clue as to his knowledge about the kind of damage we were describing. Conversely, at Body Shop B, the manager cited several examples of his experience with the kind of damage we had suffered, as well as his experience working with our insurance company. He even gave us the number to call for fast service.

5. Consistency. There is a greater potential for trust when people are consistent and predictable in performing positive behaviors. Inconsistency or a predictable pattern of negative behaviors does little to inspire trust. The employees at Body Shop A were consistent in not answering their telephone. That pattern of negative behaviors was a strike against them in terms of establishing trust. Although we had been referred by a friend, the behavior we saw was inconsistent with what our friend had explained. The employees at Body Shop B, on the other hand, told us to come right down and they would be waiting. When we arrived, we were helped immediately. And when we were promised that someone would get back to us and he did, the behavior reinforced the consistency and validated the trust.

Certainly many factors in life inspire trust, among them a perception of attentiveness, energy, openness, knowledge, and consistency. Since trust is essential to a successful self-managed work team, it is wise for each member of that team periodically to take stock of the ways to inspire trust in other team members. Good intentions are not enough. If intentions are not turned into action, then when we call on our team members to trust us, they may very well inquire as to why they should.

The following exercise will help you assess whether you inspire trust.

◇ **How Do You Inspire Trust?** ◇

Think through your own team behaviors and jot down an action for each of the following ways in which you inspire trust from your team. If you are having trouble thinking of an example, you might consider making a more deliberate or obvious effort in that area.

1. I demonstrate *attentiveness* by: _____

_____

_____

_____

_____

2. I demonstrate *energy* by: _____

_____

_____

_____

_____

3. I demonstrate *openness* by: _____

_____

_____

_____

_____

4. I demonstrate my *knowledge* of the subject by: _____

_____

_____

_____

_____

5. I demonstrate *consistency* by: _____

_____

_____

_____

_____

Giving Wings

This is a simple story
Of helping others to achieve their dreams.
It's about love and friendship;
It's not as hard as it seems.

A man was walking along the seashore,
And as he paced the sandy ground,
He stumbled upon a creature—
A bird is what he found.

He brought it home and thought that
Putting it in a cage was the thing.
But after just a little while,
The bird forgot how to sing.

The message of this story,
Whether it's your mate or your child—
If you don't let them spread their wings,
They'll lose the urge to smile.

By helping someone reach their goals,
There is no greater gift.
An impenetrable bond is created,
Giving both of you a lift.

So remember the ones you love.
And please help them to try
To be the best they're capable of
By allowing them to fly.
                                                —Christopher P Neck

5

TEAM PROBLEM SOLVING

The application of knowledge and skills to achieve democratic, creative, and effective solutions to problems faced by the team

◩ LEARNING TO DISAGREE AGREEABLY ◩

One of the most difficult challenges about working on a team is learning how to handle disagreements with other team members successfully. An important step in developing this skill is to reflect on how you would handle disagreements in specific situations. Use the following exercise to test how you would respond.

◇ A Matter of Life and Death ◇

A man's wife has a terminal disease; he loves her very much. This man has recently learned that a company developed a drug that can successfully treat the disease, but the drug is in short supply and is very expensive.

In researching the situation, the man discovers that to get the quantity his wife needs will cost $20,000. After approaching every possible source available to him (family, friends, lending institutions), he is able to raise only $12,000. In desperation, he goes to the drug company with his $12,000, but its representatives refuse the man the drug unless he pays the full $20,000.

In despair, the man breaks into the company's warehouse and steals the drug. On his way out, he leaves a check for $12,000 and a signed note committing himself to pay the remaining $8,000 to the company at the earliest possible date. Subsequently the man is arrested.

You have been selected to serve on the jury. Based on the information provided you must decide on a verdict of guilty or not guilty.

1. What is your verdict? _____

2. What is the primary reason for your verdict? _____ ___

_____

3. If you judge him guilty, recommend the type of punishment. _____

_____

Assume that another person on the jury has the opposite viewpoint of your own. During a disagreement it is usually helpful
to try to understand the other person's view before you try to
explain your own. Put yourself in his shoes. What reasons can
you think of to support this opposite view?

_____

_____

Can you think of a way that you can both reach your chosen
objective, at least in part? Explain your ideas for combining
both views into a reasonable decision. _____

_____

On a team, disagreements are inevitable, especially when
the problems are emotionally loaded and pose more than
one clear solution. How you handle these disagreements
will affect not only your team's immediate action but your
long-term ability to work together.

Here are some simple lessons to remember about disagreeing agreeably on a team:

1. Collect your thoughts and composure. Avoid the
temptation to come out slugging.

2. Try to understand the other person's position.
Why is she taking a different view?

3. Try to think of a way that you can both win, at
least in part.

4. If you can't reach a mutually agreeable solution,
consider how important this issue is to you. How certain
are you that you are right and the other person is wrong?
If you both have expressed your honest views and can't
reach agreement, you may want to go along with the other

person on this issue and save your firm stance for another issue that is more important to you.

5. Keep in mind that this difficult situation will pass and will likely be quickly forgotten, but **you and your teammate will have to work together in the future.** Remember that you are both on the same side.

◩ HOW TO TALK TO A PROBLEM ◩ TEAM MEMBER

What if a member of your team always shows up late, is not putting in his fair share of work, tells jokes that are offensive and disruptive, or has some other problem? You may not be sure how to talk to him about this, but something has to be done; this behavior is reducing the effectiveness of the team.

According to turkey experts, when a turkey is wounded and has a spot of blood on its feathers, the other turkeys will peck at that spot until they peck the wounded turkey to death. Instead of helping the turkey get rid of its problem (the wound), the fellow turkeys make it worse by pecking at it. In the same way, if a fellow team member has a problem (such as not working hard enough or showing up late for meetings), you and your fellow team members can either peck at the problem and make it worse, or you can give the member constructive feedback and support so that the team member can deal with the problem and function productively again.

Here are some tips on how to talk to team members about a problem in a constructive manner as opposed to pecking the problem and making it even bigger for your team:

1. Be specific rather than general. Give good, clear, and recent examples about the problem behavior.

2. Phrase the problem as a problem for the whole team, not just the individual. State how the problem disrupts the team. Also, show the member that the team will offer support to help the member overcome this problem area. Use *we* instead of *you*. For example, "I think we have a problem that we must work on solving together" may be more beneficial and have less likelihood of the member's becoming defensive than if you said, "I think you have a problem that you must work on solving by yourself."

3. Focus on controllable things. Your criticism should be with respect to things that a team member has control over, things that he can really do something about.

4. Give constructive criticism at a time when the team member appears most ready to accept it. For example, when the member is leaving for lunch may not be the best time to give criticism because the member is right in the middle of an important activity: going to get lunch.

5. Remember that your purpose is to improve the team member's behavior. Don't criticize to embarrass or to put someone on the spot.

6. Keep feedback professional. Don't use labels such as *stupid* or *incompetent*. Describe behaviors, and avoid the labels. For example, instead of saying, "You are a lazy bum; what are you going to do about it?" say, "You were not at the meeting we had all agreed upon holding. May we discuss this?"

7. Ensure understanding. Make sure criticism is concise and complete enough that the team member understands the problem. Having the team member rephrase the problem may be helpful.

8. Don't be a parent. Talk to the problem team member as an equal, not as a controlling parent, supervisor, or boss. State how the behaviors need correcting for the good of the team.

Finally, it is important not to lose sight of a very important item regarding feedback to teammates. Consider the following story:

This is a story of a father and his young son during a summer vacation. The son seemed to misbehave constantly, and the father seemed to be constantly rebuking and correcting him. One day later in the week, the son tried especially hard to live up to his dad's standards. In fact, he didn't do a single thing wrong that called for correcting. After he said his prayers and jumped into bed, the boy's bottom lip began to quiver. "What's the matter son?" the father asked. Barely able to speak, the boy looked with glassy eyes at his dad and asked, "Daddy, haven't I been a good boy today?"[22]

The point here is that when you communicate with a team member who is causing problems, never lose sight of the importance of praising her for the things she does well.

◪ MEETING THE CHALLENGE OF THE ◪ PROBLEM TEAM MEMBER

Usually team members are committed to helping their team succeed and are willing to work hard to achieve this goal. Sometimes, however, members let their team down, at least for awhile. Learning to deal with this situation constructively is an important part of helping your team succeed. Begin thinking about positively dealing with members who do cause problems for a team by completing the following exercise situation.

◇ Dealing With a Chronically Absent ◇ Team Member

You are about to attend a meeting of your work team. The purpose of the meeting is to discuss one of your team members, Scott, who is absent from work today. In fact, he has been absent several times over the past month, and when he has come to work, he has frequently been late. This had made life very difficult for your team since the same workload must be completed to stay on schedule despite being short one worker.

Several members have talked to Scott individually and expressed their concern about his absences and the burden it is placing on the team. One of the reasons for the problem is that Scott's wife, Anne, has been ill, and Scott has been trying to help out at home. Your team, however, believes he has been using the situation as an excuse. Today the team learned that Anne had improved enough to return to her own job a couple of days ago.

Your team must decide what action it will take, if any. You could schedule a formal counseling meeting where the whole team expresses its displeasure with Scott and gives him a warning, write up a team report documenting Scott's absences for his employment file, or take action to have Scott removed from the team, which could also lead to Scott losing his job.

Many members of your team say that Scott has already been given enough chances since they have talked to him on several occasions. Scott has been aware of his negative impact on the team for at least two weeks. Your whole team agrees that the situation can't continue much longer.

Your team has strained itself to the limit trying to cover for Scott, and it will be touch and go as to whether you reach your quarterly team objective, which directly affects your pay bonuses (the bonus can reach up to 10 percent of your pay and is based on your team's overall performance).

1. What do you believe your team should do about Scott?

_____

_____

2. Explain how your team can prevent situations like this from occurring in the future? _____

_____

_____

Here are some simple tips to remember when dealing with members who are not pulling their weight on the team:

1. Be sure that you are seeing the situation clearly. If possible, discuss your concerns with the person openly and honestly without attacking. If this is not possible, check your perceptions with other team members, but don't gossip behind the person's back.

2. Be sure that the problem team member understands the situation and the negative burden that is being placed on the team. Has the team openly, honestly, and constructively communicated the problem and its negative impact?

3. Develop an agreed-on plan that all team members think will constructively correct the problem if the problem cannot be resolved through informal conversations with the individual. The whole team should be involved in developing a constructive solution.

4. Consider the long-term effects of how you approach the problem. Try to reach a solution that fixes the situation and does not threaten the team's ability to work together over the long run. Does the strategy serve as a fair way to resolve similar problems with other team members in the future? Would you feel that you were being treated fairly if the team approached you in this way if you were in this same situation?

5. Keep the focus on the problem, not the person. The key is to correct the problem permanently in a way that is acceptable to all and not lynch the person because of the short-run inconvenience she is causing. If the problem can be corrected on an objective problem-solving basis rather than as a personal feud, the chances for long-term positive results and restored effective teamwork are much better. After all, you are all on the same team.

◤ CREATING TEAM SOLUTIONS ◤

Coming up with solutions for problems that your team is facing may seem like a difficult task. You may be feeling stressed because you and your team need to find answers to questions and solutions to problems, and you don't know where to find them. Worry no more. Often the place to find the solutions to all your team's challenges lies within your group, in the minds of your team members.

Consider the following story of a scientist, Art Fry, who worked for the 3M Company and came up with the idea for one of 3M's best-selling products:

> Every Sunday as he sang in the church choir, Fry became irritated—not from singing but because the small pieces of paper he used to mark his pages in the hymnal invariably fell out on the floor. On one particular Sunday when this happened, Fry remembered an adhesive a colleague had developed that everyone thought was a failure because it did not stick very well. Fry coated the adhesive on a small piece of paper and found that it was not only a good bookmark, but fine for writing notes. Best of all, it would stay in place as long as he wanted it to, and then he could remove it without damage to the surface it was stuck to.[23]

The resulting product was called Post-it, and it has become one of 3M's most successful office products.

What about solutions to your team's problems? Maybe your team's project is to determine a better way for the company's employees to deal with customer complaints, but you don't have a clue about where to begin. Or perhaps many team members don't seem to get along with each other, and you don't know how to resolve this problem. Whatever your problems are, you have the power right within your team to come up with creative solutions to them.

"How can we do this?" you may be asking? We believe you can develop creative solutions for the challenges your team is facing by brainstorming. Brainstorming can help your team pull out from the minds of your team members the solutions to your problems. Here is how it works:

1. Team members meet together in a room with a circular table. Each member sits at the table.

2. Someone in the group, such as the team leader, states the current problem or challenge facing the group. Everyone must agree that the problem is exactly as stated. If there is any disagreement, discussion should take place until everyone agrees.

3. Go around the table one by one, and ask each team member to throw out an idea for solving the problem or handling the challenge. Someone in the group is in charge of writing these ideas down on a large sheet of paper so that everyone can see them. Someone who does not have an idea at the time can say, "Pass."

4. Continue to go around the table until the meeting time is over or no more ideas can be generated.

It is important to follow certain rules while the idea generation is occurring:

- No criticism is allowed. No other member can say whether an idea is good or bad.
- Questions can be asked only for clarification of an idea.
- Free-wheeling is a plus. Wild and crazy ideas are welcome, and in fact they may help trigger other ideas from team members. Don't worry about whether the idea you voice is good, bad, silly, or realistic; just say it.
- Go for quantity. The more ideas you get from team members, the better that this effort will be.
- Combine and improve. It is certainly fine to build on someone else's idea.

Once time is up or no more ideas can be generated, your team will be amazed at what's in front of them: a long list of ideas to consider where earlier they were stumped about what to do. (See how neat this process is?) The team now examines the list of suggested ideas and determines which ones to consider carefully. One way to do this is to break the list up into "good," "kind-of-good," and "no way." Then your team should analyze the pared-down list with the best answers and choose which idea seems to be a solution to the problem.

◪ ARE YOUR MEETINGS A WASTE OF TIME? ◪

"There is too much time spent in team meetings." "People show up late." "The meetings seem to drag on and on, and nothing ever seems to get accomplished." Do these complaints sound familiar? Are you feeling frustrated by the numerous team meetings that you have to attend? Do you too feel that many of these meetings are useless because nothing ever seems to get done, they drag on and on, and people are always showing up late? If you answered yes to any of these questions, then this unit can help.

Team meetings, done right, can help your team solve problems, communicate with each other, and even provide emotional support. If your team meetings seem like a mess, there is good news. There are several things within your team's control that you can do to help your meetings be more productive. Consider these guidelines for helping you make your team meetings more enjoyable and productive for you and your team members:

1. Set a purpose before the meeting. An effective meeting is one that achieves its purpose. The purpose is what you expect to accomplish by the end of the meeting or your reason for meeting.

2. Don't meet just for the sake of meeting, without a purpose. This would be a waste of everyone's time.

3. Once the purpose is established, all team members should ask themselves, **"Is there another way to achieve the purpose without holding a team meeting?"** For example, would a memo, e-mail, or fax achieve the same purpose more efficiently? If the answer to this question is yes, then holding a meeting in this situation would probably be a waste of time.

4. Set an agenda. An agenda can help the team save time by not going off on tangents. An agenda should include what the team will discuss at the meeting in order to achieve the stated meeting purpose. If possible, prepare the agenda ahead of time, and invite all team members to contribute items for the agenda.

5. Distribute the agenda early so that everyone can be prepared for the discussion.

6. Stay on track during the meeting. Make a special effort to follow the agenda.

7. Set a time limit for the meeting and hold to it. This time limit should be long enough to discuss all agenda items thoroughly.

8. Set an exact time for the meeting to begin and end. Don't punish those who arrive on time by making them wait for those who don't. Starting late rewards the sloppy behavior of being late; don't lightly excuse or condone lateness by team members.

9. Decide how to deal with lateness. For example, make a rule that whoever is late has to buy the rest of the team coffee and doughnuts for the next meeting.

10. Designate a record keeper to keep concise notes at the meeting. The notes, or minutes, should be distributed soon after the meeting to all team members so that everyone can ensure the accuracy of what was discussed and who was responsible for what.

11. Be prepared to discuss the items on the agenda. All team members should take an active role in discussing these agenda items during the meeting.

12. Encourage all members to communicate during meetings. Statements like, "How do you feel about this?" or "We have not heard from you yet" may help generate discussion.

13. Encourage the airing of all views, even ones that may conflict with others. Only by hearing all sides of an issue can your team reach the best decision possible.

14. Stop the meeting when all agenda items have been discussed. Those who want to stay and chat can do so; those who need to get to other things can leave.

15. Every member in the team has a part in making the team meeting a success. It is everyone's responsibility to make sure the meetings are beneficial and not a waste of time, and it is everyone's responsibility to make sure that these guidelines are followed.

16. Practice, practice, practice. Successful team meetings don't just happen. It takes a lot of hard work to make your meeting work for you and your team. Continue practicing these guidelines, and your meetings will be productive and help you and your team work smarter and better.

◪ YOUR TEAM'S TIME IS YOUR BUSINESS ◪

Stanley Marcus, the legendary retailer and former chairman of the board of Neiman-Marcus, was once asked, "What do the most successful people you know have in common?" He replied, "They all have 24-hour days. . . . The world has expanded in almost all directions, but we still have a 24-hour day. The most successful people and most unsuccessful people all receive the same ration of hours each day." [24]

His message is that the difference between being successful and not being successful depends on how you use your daily ration of twenty-four hours. This applies not only to individuals but to your team.

Your team time management involves two questions:

"What is the best use of *my* time?" and "What is the best use of *our* time?"

Why is team time management so important? The reason is quite simple: Your team has only a limited amount of time to complete the project at hand. Given the enormous pressures existing in your organization to perform well at the lowest cost possible, time used wisely means better performance for your team and your organization. It's your business at stake.

Imagine for a moment that your team had only a bag of twenty-four crackers to satisfy your members' hunger for an entire day. What would you do? Probably you'd guard those crackers, and be very careful not to waste them. Perhaps you'd devise a plan to allocate the crackers to minimize your team members' hunger so they can perform effectively. In reality, each day your team is given a small bag of a valuable yet scarce resource: time. In this bag, there are only twenty-four hours. In order to get through the day productively, you must manage your bag of time wisely. Here are some guidelines to help your team manage its precious time:

1. Recognize that your team's time is a scarce commodity. It is valuable and can't be wasted. If your team distortedly views time as a never-ending supply, it will not be motivated to practice effective time management.

2. Write down your team's goals.

3. Create a "to-do" list of the tasks that your team needs to perform. Rank the tasks on the list in terms of their importance. For example, place an *A* next to the tasks that are the most important, a *B* next to the lesser important items, and a *C* next to the least important items. If your team is spending time doing some activity that is not a high priority, then you're probably wasting time.

4. Arrange your work area in an orderly manner. This can be a powerful team time tactic. If your work area is a mess, your team members will waste time looking for necessary items such as papers, files, or tools.

5. Find hidden time. If your team reaches a standstill for some reason—perhaps it needs more resources or some key member is missing—use this time wisely instead of sitting around. Organize your work setting or gather important job-related information.

6. Focus your team's physical and mental energy on the task at hand. If your team members use their physical and mental energy on multiple nonpriority issues, completing the assigned project will take longer.

7. Pace yourself. The team should strive to establish a set routine for performing tasks. Routine creates habits in the way your team works and helps members know in advance what is required and what needs to be done.

8. Take advantage of team peaks. Learn to recognize when your team's peak performance times occur, such as early morning or late afternoon. Use them to accomplish your most demanding tasks during those times.

The following exercise is designed to help your team established priorities and avoid time-busting activities.

◇ **Establishing Team Priorities** ◇

In the space provided on the facing page, list activities your team has spent time performing during the past week. Next is the "importance" column; place an **A** next to the tasks that are most important, a **B** next to the items that are not as important as **A** items, or a **C** next to items that rank low in priority. One way to decide on the importance of tasks is to subject the individual activities to intense questioning—for example:

- Will it help us reach an important team goal?

- Does it have a specific deadline?

- Is it an order from someone the team can't ignore, like the CEO or a customer?

Ranking of Team Tasks

Team Tasks Normally Performed	Rank	Reason for the Rank

- Will it advance our team's standing in the organization, or will doing this hurt us?

- Will it make us more knowledgeable or help us to fulfill our potential?

- Will it matter a year from now?

- Will it really matter if we don't do it?

- Is it important to someone we really care about?

In the last column, specify why the group ranked it as it did.

When you've completed this exercise, your team will be one step closer to effective team time management. You should now realize what tasks you should spend your valuable team time performing and what tasks to put at the bottom of the list.

Perform this exercise periodically as your team achieves the established goals or when you want to set new ones. Note that not achieving your goals may be a signal to perform this exercise.

◪ PREPARING A RIGHT PATH ◪

"Our team is split on what we should do. About half of the members believe it is all right to use a less expensive material to produce our product—though it will probably reduce the durability of it and thus shorten the product's life. These members feel the use of this alternative material will make our team look good in the eyes of management because our production costs would now be less than those of all the other teams. I'm confused about what we should do."

What should this team do? Before we address this question, let's examine the story on page 143.

A young carpenter married a building contractor's daughter. Soon thereafter, the father-in-law decided to boost the career of his new son-in-law. "Son," he said, "I don't want you to start at the bottom of this construction business as I did. I want you to go out to my job-site and build the most tremendous house this town has ever seen. Put the best of everything in it, make it a showplace, and turn it over to me when you are finished."

"Well, this is an opportunity to make a killing," thought the son-in-law. He hurried out to slap together a building that would survive two fairly stiff gales. He made a deal with a shady wholesaler and installed substandard lumber, shingles, cinder blocks, cement, etc., but billed for the best materials. The two cheats split the profits from their deception. In short order the son-in-law presented his father-in-law with the keys to the newly finished house.

"Is it a tremendous showplace of the newest and best materials as I asked?" inquired the father-in-law.

"It sure is, Dad," answered the son-in-law.

"Is it the finest house ever built, son?"

"You betcha, Dad."

"All right, where's the final bill? And did you include a good profit in it for yourself?"

"Uh, well . . . here it is," the son-in-law replied, "and yes, I did."

"OK, let me write out a check. Do you have the deed with you?"

As he accepted the deed, the father-in-law said, "I didn't tell you why I wanted that house to be the best ever built. I wanted it to be something special that I could give to you and my daughter to show you how much I love you. Here, take the deed and the keys. Go live in that showplace; it's yours now. Go live in the house you built—for yourself!"

The young man slinked away, shattered and frustrated.
He thought he was making a fortune at his father-in-
law's expense by shaving money here and there with
inferior materials and various shortcuts, but in the end
he only cheated himself.[25]

The son-in-law was obviously faced with a precarious
decision here, and I'm sure many of you would agree that
he probably did not make the right decision by choosing
to cheat his father-in-law. In the long run, he ended up
cheating himself.

As team members, you will no doubt be confronted
with situations that pose similar decisions of choosing
right and wrong, and short-term gains versus long-term
costs. In other words, you and your fellow team members
will have to face decisions involving *ethics*, the rules that
guide us through situations where different alternatives to
solutions or conflicting interests exist. Ethical decisions are
those that guide us to make choices that promote moral
outcomes, such as promise keeping, nonviolence, helping
others, showing respect for others, and showing respect
for others' property.

Ethical actions by your team are important to its long-
term success. There is a myth that organizations and teams
that act ethically have lower performance levels (e.g.,
profits). This may be true in the short run, but businesses
and teams that engage in unethical practices make themselves vulnerable to legal suits and loss of reputation. In
fact, in the long run, a team's ethical decisions will benefit
the team by building trust and respect among all team
members and between the team as a whole and all organization members and customers.

Making the right decision is not always easy and
clear-cut. Here are some questions to help you decide
whether an action is ethical:

1. **The Golden Rule.** Are you treating others as you
   would want to be treated?

2. **Publicity.** Would you be comfortable if your reasoning and your decision were to be publicized on the front page of the *New York Times*, *USA Today*, or your community's newspaper?
3. **Kid on your shoulder.** Would you be comfortable if your children (or brother or sister) were observing you? Is your behavior an example of ethical behavior?

If your team answered yes to these three questions, it's fairly safe to say that your team's potential action will be an ethical one; it is morally correct and will probably promote at least some of the moral outcomes we discussed.

◣ WHERE DOES YOUR TEAM WANT TO GO? ◣

It is futile to exert effort with no direction. Imagine for a moment that your entire team decided to take a trip together, and you all piled into a large van. You were selected to be the driver, so you start the automobile and head to the nearest highway. Everyone in the van is happy and smiling until about an hour later when someone remarks, "Where are we going?" You reply, "I don't know." Other members just shrug their shoulders. After a few more minutes, some bickering erupts among team members because someone wants to go to city A, while someone else wants to go to city B. Amid all of the noise and chaos, you think to yourself, "Wow, this mess could have been easily avoided if we had reached a mutually agreed destination before we left."

Every day your team "travels" together; your "traveling" is working together as a unified group. Do you know what you are working toward? In other words, do you know your team's destination? Or is your team traveling together without a clear picture of where you are actually going and what you are trying to achieve?

The story illustrates what can happen to your team in its daily activities if it fails to set a destination in terms of what the group wants to achieve. Your group destination is your team goal. The dictionary defines a goal as "the *result* toward which effort is directed." What is the result in which your team's effort is directed? In other words, what are the *goals* of your team?

Successful teams don't travel together unless they have a specific destination, a specific goal. If your team doesn't have specific goals, you never get anywhere. So get together with your team and determine what you want to accomplish. Set goals. Here are some tips to help you:

1. Conduct a team examination. Before your team can establish specific goals, the members need to discuss what's important to them and what they'd like to accomplish. The team must truly want to accomplish the team-set goals, so everyone must value the team's final destination. (The following team goal-setting exercise might help you with this point.)

2. Avoid fuzzy goals; be specific. If your team says, "We'll someday be the best team in the company," you might have a goal but it's not very likely to happen. The problem is the *someday*. It's fuzzy, unclear, and nonspecific. Your team goal needs to be specific. *When* are you going to be the best team? *What* does "best" mean? *How* are you going to do this? If your goals are more specific, it paints a more vivid picture of your team's destination and will make it easier to get there.

3. Set long-term and short-term goals. Your team's goals need to focus on both the long run and the short run. If your team decides on a long-term goal of becoming the top-performing team in the company, it needs to accomplish short-range goals to get there—for example, "All team members will learn new skills." Another way of looking at this is to imagine your team's long-term goal of writing a book. In order to do this, your team could set a short-term goal of writing five pages a day. Short-term goals help your team accomplish its long-term destination.

◇ **Team Goal Setting** ◇

Answer the following questions to help you set long-term and short-term goals.

Long-Term Team Goals
What do your team members value most (e.g., producing the most; producing the best quality; becoming friends with all team members)? What would your team most like to accomplish during its time together? An interesting way to approach this question is to ask each individual member to draw a picture (artistic quality is not important) of what he or she values most. Then post all of the pictures on the wall to see if the pictures could possibly be combined to form one "team" picture. This final picture could serve as an illustration of your team's long-term goals.

Short-Term Team Goals
What does your team need to do now in order to make its picture come true?

_____

_____

_____

_____

Seize the Day

Carpe Diem,
Is what I say.
In other words,
Seize the day.

To make it simpler,
I will relay.
"Gather Ye Rosebuds,
While Ye May."

Consider this simple scenario,
Ponder it for a while.
Hopefully, it will make you think;
And maybe change your style.

If you were given 24 gold coins,
To spend each day as you choose,
But when the day is up—the ones you didn't spend,
You'd completely lose.

Your actions in this situation,
Shouldn't require you to stall.
Of course you would reply,
"I wouldn't save any at all."

In our real lives, this actually does occur.
This truly does transpire.
We're given 24 golden hours each day,
To use any way we desire.

But many times, we don't use them wisely;
Commonplace—is how they appear.
We treat them as if we truly believe,
We can save them for sometime next year.

But once the day is finished,
No matter your chosen endeavor,
No one can ever retrieve it.
An hour lost—is gone forever.

The message in these basic words,
Is don't waste your coins away.
Always give it all you've got.
Carpe Diem—Seize the Day!
                    —Christopher P. Neck

6

TEAM PLAY

An exercise in the right to fun while strengthening team relationships

Team Play is an opportunity for team members to get to know each other better as they make play of their work. The processes used in this exercise are team decision making, communicating, problem solving, and team building. The objective is for team members to have fun as they develop their team skills and comraderie. Each team member needs a copy of Team Play to participate.

There are four steps to this exercise. Step 1 is the reading or role playing of the case, "Your Team's Dream Vacation." Step 2 asks team members to develop dream descriptions for their favorite activities on the "Recreation Activities List." In Step 3, team members develop both personal and team itineraries for the five-day vacation. A final rating of the Team Play experience is completed in Step 4.

This exercise can be used by a small team of three to five or in multiple teams of three or four members. If more than one team participates, a facilitator of the larger group may do the following:

1. Deal with the issue of team selection. Decide whether team members should self-select (ask team members to choose those they would like to get to know better) or whether you should randomly assign team membership. Wait until the teams are formed before handing out the exercise.

2. Role play the character of the CEO in Step 1, "Your Team's Dream Vacation."

3. Clarify instructions for each step you include in the exercise.

4. Collect all individual team rating responses in Step 4, develop a large-group tally, and report back to everyone.

5. Lead a final large-group discussion and debriefing. Evaluate the overall process. Was it fun? Was it stressful? Was any part difficult to complete? Why? How many would really want to go on a five-day dream vacation with their team members?

Step 1: Your Team's Dream Vacation

Instructions: Read the following scenario and imagine that you are a group participant at a private resort island.

> You and the other members of your group arrive Sunday night at a private resort island, summoned there by the newly appointed CEO of your organization for what is described as an important meeting
>
> At the appointed meeting time, you find yourself seated at a large round table nestled by an imposing fireplace. In front of you is a folder labeled, "Briefing File: Do Not Open Until Instructed to Do So." A door opens, the CEO enters the room, walks over to the crackling fire, and begins to describe the purpose of the meeting.
>
> "You are my key leadership team and I am going to rely heavily on you as I try to have a positive influence in my new leadership role. I am aware that you are highly trained and competent individuals. However, I want you to be a solid team, not just a collection of independent performers.
>
> "I am aware that you have been working very long hours over the past few months as our organization has attempted to roll out its new competitive strategy. You have done your individual jobs well, and for the most

part the strategy is in place. Now for the purpose of this gathering: For the next five days you will be [*in a loud voice for emphasis*] ON VACATION!" The CEO is now smiling.

"Now please open your folders. You will notice that the contents include a list of numerous recreation activities and a five-day planning sheet. For the remainder of the evening you need to make decisions about what you will be doing during your vacation over the next five days. You can choose three activities per day: one in the morning, one in the afternoon, and one in the evening. This gives you fifteen time slots. You can repeat activities as often as you want. If you choose to attend one of the island's several five-star gourmet restaurants, that will be your activity for that time slot. Otherwise you will have shorter meals in the hotel's standard restaurant café serving basic American cuisine, thus allowing you time for a separate activity. Note also that some of the activities can be enjoyed only during the day or during the evening."

"Oh, by the way, there is one other requirement: you do all your activities together. For example, if golf is chosen as an activity for a given time slot, then everyone must participate. I want you to get to know each other better and to become a more cohesive team, so you are to play together all week. Now plan your vacation. Your primary task will be to create the vacation itinerary that your entire group agrees to participate in."

Step 2: Recreation Activities List

Break into teams of three or four. Each member of the team chooses two or three of the activities listed on pages 153 and 154 and writes a short "dream" description for those activities. Here is an example for golf: Play golf on one of the three professional-quality golf courses. Top-of-the-line equipment will be provided for each player. All three of the beautiful courses were recently ranked as one of the

(*Text continues on page 155.*)

amusement park _____

casino gambling _____

free time _____

hang gliding _____

archaeological dig _____

concert _____

game room _____

health spa _____

biking _____

deep sea fishing _____

golf _____

helicopter ride _____

bungee jumping _____

flying lesson _____

gourmet cooking lesson _____

hiking _____

horseback riding

movie premier

professional development seminar

shopping

swimming pool

water skiing, jet skiing

tour and swim coral reef

hot air balloon ride

recreational reading

tennis

wilderness jeep tour

island tour

restaurant dining

tour a brewery or winery

luau

top fifty most enjoyable golf courses in the world in *Golf Magazine*. A brief lesson with a former U.S. Open and Masters champion will immediately precede your round of golf.

When you are done, take turns reading aloud to your group the descriptions. A time limit of about fifteen minutes is suggested. When you have completed this, move on to Step 3: Planning the Itinerary.

Step 3: Planning the Itinerary

Fill in your individual choices for your vacation using the "Individual" column. You will have approximately five to ten minutes to complete this.

Next, each team member summarizes the content of his or her itinerary. You may want to talk about why you chose the activities and your logic for organizing them as you did. This should take about ten to fifteen minutes.

Finally, discuss and decide on a team vacation itinerary that the entire group agrees to. Record your choices in the "Team" column. Remember that all team members must participate together on each activity of the team itinerary.

	Individual	Team
Monday		
Morning	_____	_____
Afternoon	_____	_____
Evening	_____	_____
Tuesday		
Morning	_____	_____
Afternoon	_____	_____
Evening	_____	_____
Wednesday		
Morning	_____	_____
Afternoon	_____	_____
Evening	_____	_____

Thursday

   Morning   _____   _____

   Afternoon   _____   _____

   Evening   _____   _____

Friday

   Morning   _____   _____

   Afternoon   _____   _____

   Evening   _____   _____

Step 4: Rating Your Experience

This is a way for you and your team members to reflect on your reactions and feelings about this exercise. Complete your ratings and compare your responses with your group members.

How satisfied are you with your individual and team vacation itineraries? Below, circle the number that best describes your level of satisfaction.

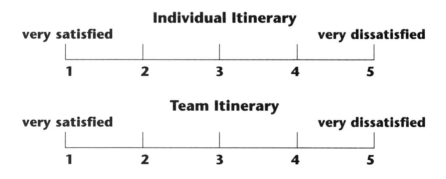

How much did your team choices change from your original individual choices? Circle the number below that best describes how much your choices changed.

NOTES

1. B. Tuckman and M. Jensen, "Stages of Small-Group Development," *Group and Organizational Development* 2 (1977): 419–427.

2. This poem was adapted from "Catching the Wind." All of the poems in this book were originally published in C. Neck, *Medicine for the Mind: Healing Words to Help You Soar* (New York: McGraw-Hill, 1995).

3. G. VanEkeren, *The Speaker's Sourcebook* (Englewood Cliffs, NJ: Prentice Hall, 1988).

4. W. Hill, "My Wife and My Mother-in-Law," *Puck* (November 6, 1915):11.

5. VanEkeren, *The Speaker's Sourcebook.*

6. B. Cavanaugh, *More Sower's Seeds* (Mahwah, NJ: Paulist Press, 1992).

7. See L. Janis, *Groupthink* (Boston: Houghton Mifflin, 1983). For further discussion of teamthink and its relation to groups see C. Manz and C. Neck, "Teamthink: Beyond the Groupthink Syndrome in Self-Managing Work Teams," *Journal of Managerial Psychology* 10 (1995): 7–15.

8. E. Chapman, *Your Attitude Is Showing: A Primer of Human Relations* (Englewood Cliffs, NJ: Prentice Hall, 1993).

9. The concepts of the Strongman, Transactor, Visionary Hero, and SuperLeader have been written about extensively elsewhere by Henry P. Sims, Jr., and Charles C. Manz. For a more detailed treatment of these ideas see C. Manz and H. Sims, Jr., *Company of Heroes* (New York: Wiley, 1996).

10. This exercise is adapted from C. Manz, M. Muto, and H. Sims, Jr., "Super Leadership Creates New Perspective for Managers," *Journal for Quality and Participation* (1990): 12–15.

11. For more information on SuperLeadership, see C. Manz and H. Sims, Jr., *SuperLeadership: Leading Others to Lead Themselves* (New York: Berkley, 1990), and Sims and Manz, *Company of Heroes.*

12. W. Piper, *Little Engine That Could* (New York: Platt & Munk, 1976).

13. Cavanaugh, *More Sower's Seeds.*

14. J. Canfield and M. Hansen, *A Third Serving of Chicken Soup for the Soul* (Deerfield Beach, FL: Health Communications, 1996).

15. D. Chopra, *Magical Mind, Magical Body* (Niles, IL: Nightingale Conant Corp., 1991).

16. This quiz is adapted from material in B. Reinhold, *Toxic Work: How to Overcome Stress, Overload, and Burnout and Revitalize Your Career* (New York: Dutton, 1996).

17. These ten modes of thought are based on material in D. Burns, *Feeling Good: The New Mood Therapy* (New York: Morrow, 1980).

18. This exercise is based on Manz, *Mastering Self-Leadership* (Englewood Cliffs, NJ: Prentice Hall, 1992).

19. Concepts of assertiveness are discussed in depth in S. Bower and G. Bower, *Asserting Yourself: A Practical Guide for Positive Change* (New York: Addison-Wesley, 1976).

20. These principles are based on a humanistic model of communication described in J. Devito, *The Interpersonal Communication Book* (New York: HarperCollins, 1995).

21. The key concepts of dealing with defensiveness were originally discussed in J. Gibb, "Defensive Communication," *Journal of Communication* 11 (1961): 141–148.

22. VanEkeren, *The Speaker's Sourcebook.*

23. Ibid.

24. B. Griessman, *Time Tactics of Very Successful People* (New York: McGraw-Hill, 1994).

25. B. Cavanaugh, *Fresh Packet of Flower Seeds* (Mahwah, NJ: Paulist Press, 1994).

INDEX

YOUR TEAM OF AUTHORS

Charles C. Manz is professor of management at Arizona State University. In fall 1997 he will be the Charles and Janet Nirenberg Professor of Business Leadership at the University of Massachusetts. He received the prestigious Marvin Bower Fellowship at the Harvard Business School in 1988–1989. His previous books include *Company of Heroes* (Wiley, 1996), *Business Without Bosses* (Wiley, 1993), and *SuperLeadership* (Berkley, 1990), all coauthored with Henry P. Sims; and *Mastering Self-Leadership* (Prentice Hall, 1992). Dr. Manz has served as a consultant and speaker on leadership, self-management, and work teams for many organizations, including Fortune 500 companies.

    Christopher P. Neck is an assistant professor of management at Virginia Polytechnic Institute and State University, where he teaches a course in management principles to over 600 students each semester. He is the author of the inspirational book *Medicine for the Mind: Healing Words to Help You Soar* (McGraw-Hill, 1996). His research interests focus on self-leadership, leadership, self-managing teams, and group decision making. Dr. Neck is an empowered speaker and consultant to many organizations. He is also an avid runner and has completed twelve marathons.

    James Mancuso has been in the business of communication for thirty years. He has been a communication consultant, industrial trainer, and college professor. His areas of expertise focus on presentational speaking, group interaction, conflict resolution, interpersonal skills, problem solving, and listening dynamics. He is the chair of the Speech Communication Department, Mesa Community College in Mesa, Arizona.

Karen P. Manz is a writer, researcher, and adult educator. She has studied groups and organizations in the public and private sectors. Her interest in teams revolves around group identity and community formation. She serves as a consultant for Manz and Associates.